VIBRATIONS:
IMPROVING YOUR PSYCHIC ENVIRONMENT

Books by Daniel Logan

THE RELUCTANT PROPHET
DO YOU HAVE ESP?
YOUR EASTERN STAR
AMERICA BEWITCHED
THE ANATOMY OF PROPHECY
VIBRATIONS: IMPROVING YOUR PSYCHIC ENVIRONMENT

VIBRATIONS:
IMPROVING YOUR PSYCHIC ENVIRONMENT
by DANIEL LOGAN

PRENTICE-HALL, INC.
Englewood Cliffs, New Jersey

Vibrations:
Improving Your Psychic Environment
by Daniel Logan

Printed in the United States of America

Prentice-Hall International, Inc., London
Prentice-Hall of Australia, Pty. Ltd., Sydney
Prentice-Hall of Canada, Ltd., Toronto
Prentice-Hall of India Private Ltd., New Delhi
Prentice-Hall of Japan, Inc., Tokyo

10 9 8 7 6 5 4 3 2 1

Library of Congress Cataloging
in Publication Data
Logan, Daniel.
    Vibrations: improving your psychic environment.
    Includes index.
    1. Psychical research. 2. Occult sciences.
I. Title.
    BF1031.L774   133.8   75-45412
    ISBN 0-13-941666-8

*This book is dedicated with
much love to
Clara Mae Aitken
and
Ruth and Albert Holumzer
whose positive vibrations
have always been of
great help to me in my life.*

CONTENTS

*Any local agitation shakes
the whole universe.
The distant effects are minute,
but they are there.*
—Alfred North Whitehead

*The aura is the emanation
that arises from the
very vibratory influences of
an individual,
mentally and spiritually—
especially from the spiritual forces.*
—Edgar Cayce (Trance #319-2)

Introduction

The bright warm sun and invigorating ocean breezes, combined with the captivating felicity of the islanders, had thrown me into a state of near euphoria. It was the first time that I had been able to relax in months. I ambled happily down the dusty, unpaved streets of the small island where I had come to rest and rejuvenate. Every person I passed smiled at me in greeting. I had succumbed to the peaceful ease and tranquillity of the remote Harbour Island in the Bahamas. The rushed, overanxious, overworked person I had become in New York City seemed to exist no more—at least not for the duration of my stay in the wondrous Caribbean.

I recall thinking that the prevailing calm and complete serenity were so manifest in the atmosphere that I could almost physically touch, not sense, them. No one even *walked* fast on Harbour Island. If someone became tired, a short nap alongside the road would soon refresh him. Twenty-five-miles-an-hour road signs indicated the top speed at which the few vehicles on the island were permitted to travel. The entire population, in fact, seemed hypnotized by their place in the sun. The children of Harbour Island were the most beautiful I had ever seen in my extensive travels; they wore constant expressions of a joy as contagious as their music, which was forever being played on instruments, listened to via radio, or vociferously sung on the streets.

The evening before I had attended a service at a local church; sort of a holy-roller type ceremony. The congregation, myself included, had prayed aloud, shouted hymns, and even danced in the aisles. We praised the Lord and each other. The emotional fever rose to such a high pitch that everyone present—even tourists who had come to gawk—were overpowered by it. Never before or since that evening have I witnessed a religious service that was more spiritual in the complete sense of the word. All of us in that church had been elevated to another state of consciousness, so powerful one could almost float on the electriclike emanations.

Immediately following that uplifting experience, I pursued some of the exalted throng to the local cinema, movies shown on sheets that had been put up in a makeshift building with no roof. After the films, a native man and his wife invited me for tea and biscuits in their home, one of the shacklike houses that dot the island.

It was at least 2 A.M. when I finally left for my room in the small guest house where I had been staying. I was not at all afraid in a place that was strange to me; one that was populated by persons of another race. It was odd because when living in New York City, I had become wary of merely going out the front door of my apartment building in the middle of the afternoon.

When I arrived at the guest house, I didn't even bother to close the door to my room. I fell asleep, and the joy and contentment I had been experiencing continued in the dream state of consciousness—vivid, detailed accounts of the preceding day's events.

Harbour Island was quite isolated when I visited

the Bahamas in 1969. One had to take a plane to the neighboring island of Eleuthera and endure a most uncomfortable boat ride. I have since heard that an airport was being built on Harbour Island, and I fear that with modernization, many of the extraordinarily positive and quite natural characteristics of the islanders will most probably disappear, as has been the case where "civilization" has encroached upon previously "backward" areas of the globe.

Economically and socially, the Harbour Islanders were not well off compared to those who lived elsewhere in the Bahamas. The natives were mostly very poor. Much of their food was taken from the sea or grown on their land. For their meager incomes they depended on the few hotels and visits from tourists. Education was minimal, and a sense of grooming and the finer social attitudes left something to be desired. On the other hand, crime of any type was practically nonexistent. In place of outwardly imposed moral and social attitudes, the people on Harbour Island had real attributes of honesty, brotherly love, and respect for nature and one another and a seemingly deeper relationship with a higher spiritual force, or God, than most communities I have yet visited.

Consciously or unconsciously, the Harbour Islanders had created a most positive psychic environment in which to live. They combined Christianity's beliefs with their own ritualistic history, forming a harmonious bridge between the teachings of Christ and their intrinsic understanding of nature and the supernatural. They are an emotional people and openly express feelings of joy or sorrow. It was not uncommon to see an adult islander jump into the air with childlike glee, cry out in grief, or quietly sit by the ocean in a form of meditation.

It is this freedom from any social and material drive, as well as the ability to express emotion without embarrassment, and the positiveness they create in their daily life that surround these people and their homeland with an aura of happiness that reaches out to visitors. Strolling around Harbour island, one cannot help but be filled with a feeling of joy, love, and friendship. Their psychic vibrations are indeed highly evolved. Only in the most remote sections of Japan did I find any other people who emanated such strong, positive vibrations.

From this experience I began to realize how modern-day man has forfeited positive, constructive vibratory auras in exchange for his so-called progress, which is merely materialistic. While on Harbour Island I dropped my guard, let it all hang out as it were, expressing feelings of joy and love of fellowman much easier than I do ordinarily. I attempted to take this feeling with me, to bring the vibrations I had become a part of on Harbour Island to my home in New York. Alas, being subject to the larger percentage of vibrations that are enforced at a place, I found it impossible and most frustrating to try to utilize these positive vibrations for any length of time.

It is amazing how quickly one does adapt to a prevailing energy level and become a part of that energy. Unfortunately, the majority rules. On the way back to New York, I stopped for a few days at Nassau, the main tourist island in the Bahamas. The difference between the natives of Nassau and those on Harbour Island is so vast that one would not believe that the islands are geographically close and that the natives share the some historical background.

The people on Nassau had tasted the fruits of material gain and expressed themselves accordingly. They are mainly interested in dealing with the thousands of tourists who disembark on their shores daily. Catering to them in every conceivable manner had left an indelible mark on the natives. They seemed suspicious, mistrustful, and in many ways, quite disagreeable. Some of them were involved in the inevitable black versus white political power struggle. In Nassau, one necessarily did lock his door behind him.

These people were victims of the vibrations of alien white men who had come to create a vacation land for themselves amidst the tropical beauty of Nassau. Gambling is one of the main attractions here. Along with it came dishonesty, crime, prostitution, and a general rip-off attitude of the tourists. I couldn't help but think that only a few hundred years ago the natives of Nassau must have expressed the very same positive vibrations that I found on Harbour Island. It was most disconcerting.

Then I was afforded an even bigger cultural jolt. I boarded a jet for home and landed at New York's

Kennedy Airport a few hours later. Besides the culture shock of being in two completely different societies in one day, I was confronted with the negative vibrations expressed by those who live and work in a large modern city.

The cabdriver who took me from the airport to my Manhattan apartment didn't speak but once on the trip, nor did he turn around. However, the negative vibrations that he gave off while driving were definite, unrelenting, and overpowering. It's my imagination, I hoped inwardly. However, he confirmed my ability to pick up on his vibrations when I gave him a twenty-dollar bill to cover the fare.

"How the hell am I supposed to give you any change?" He turned and scowled through the dirty plastic window that protects drivers from passengers in New York City. (I'm the one who needs the protection, I recall thinking that day.) "Lousy twenty-dollar bills. The last guy gave me a twenty. They always give me a twenty when I first get on work! You get out and change it in a store yourself. And leave your luggage here till you get back. I've been ripped off too many times lately." The fare, by the way, came to eleven dollars.

The doorman in my building had low vibrations, which I attribute to his doing a job he detested—quite the norm for many who work in a large city. His hatred of his job was even more apparent to me since I had been gone for three weeks. It's amazing what one can get used to, put up with, or otherwise shrug off when there is no alternative.

In the first few days that I was back, I could not cope with the vibrations of the majority of people I had to confront. I was literally overpowered by the vibrations that emanated from them. I had been witness to the antithesis of negation on Harbour Island, and I now felt as though I might just as well have been on another planet. For almost a week, I became a hermit, going out only when necessary, being with people only when I had to. It was a sad comment on the place where I lived. Shortly afterward I moved out of the city altogether.

It was this trip to Harbour Island and the shocking return home that initiated my interest in the theory that the vibrations of geographic locations as well as objects and persons can be psychometrized. Questions began to form in my head that were not there before the trip: Why were the natives of Harbour Island on an apparently different level of consciousness from their compatriots on Nassau? Why was a woman whom I befriended on Harbour Island filled with such love and joy even though she was living in abject poverty, making a meager living weaving inexpensive reed baskets? And why did my doorman, who was paid rather well and tipped exceedingly well, constantly register negative vibrations?

Was it the city that was responsible for creating the negative vibrations of people? Or was it vice versa—were people who vibrated in negative ways attracted to a city, bringing down the general level of vibratory energy to such a low ebb?

These questions opened up a psychic investigation that was to prove to me that people who live in specific geographic locations emanate completely different vibrations from those who dwell elsewhere. And, in many instances, when a person relocates, his aura and his vibrations change as well.

Lately there has been much talk and many books about changing one's life through psychical or mental attitudes. But what of changing the psychic vibrations that surround each of us as individuals? I believe that it is possible to build up certain psychic vibrations around yourself which will induce a correct level of awareness for your own individual soul evolvement. I would like to share what I found, to assist those who might need some new direction, some proper alignment with their own psychic environment.

A Room
Not Quite
One's Own

In 1973 Elizabeth Towland was thirty years old. She was a secretary and lived with a younger sister in an apartment complex outside of Fort Lee, New Jersey.

Elizabeth Towland had not married, because as she put it, "I guess I'm too demanding of perfection. The guy would have to have the looks of Rock Hudson, the personality of Johnny Carson, and the brains of Henry Kissinger!"

In April 1973 Elizabeth's sister, Julie, got married and moved to the West Coast, where her husband had a real estate business. Elizabeth found that she could no longer manage the rental of the apartment that she had shared with Julie. She proceeded with the tedious chore of searching for a place to live. And it was the same with apartments as it was with prospective husbands—Elizabeth was far too choosy.

"It's not big enough" would be the way she got out of signing a lease for an apartment that she could afford. And this one is too far from the transit system, she'd rationalize to herself after turning another apartment down. Elizabeth exhausted herself for several weekends in her unsuccessful quest for a new home.

One late Saturday afternoon, having spent the entire day and all her energy looking through newspaper advertisements and answering the ones she thought might fit her specifications, Elizabeth rang the superintendent's bell of a building listed in a local New Jersey newspaper.

"I'd like to see the apartment you have for rent," Elizabeth said to the woman who answered the door.

"It isn't very big." The woman's response was oddly negative. "How many are you?"

"There's just me."

"No roommates, or anything?"

"No, just me." Elizabeth was becoming annoyed at the woman's line of questioning.

"Okay, I'll show it to you." Reluctantly, the woman took out her passkey and led Elizabeth to the elevator. Anything seemed a bother for the hefty, unkempt woman. "The rooms are on the fourth floor," she sighed.

As she entered apartment 4D, Elizabeth felt a strong, immediate response. A huge picture window was directly in front of her, and since the building was located high up on the Palisades overlooking the Hudson River, the view of New York City was breathtaking. A large fern planted in a wicker basket was in front of the window. It was the only thing in the entire apartment. Elizabeth was an amateur horticulturist and ferns were a particular favorite of hers. Maybe it's a good sign, she thought to herself.

The apartment was not too different from the ones she had been seeing; what is ludicrously advertised as two and a half rooms and in actuality amounts to one large L-shaped room (the alcove of which can be sectioned off to make a small sleeping area), a very small dressing area in front of the bathroom, and a kitchenette.

The apartment had been painted beige, a color Elizabeth was fond of. She immediately felt at home, very comfortable. Elizabeth asked the slovenly woman about the rent and other financial terms. This done, they went down to the superintendent's ground-floor apartment, and without further delay, Elizabeth signed the lease.

"And what's so special about this place?" Elizabeth's mother inquired when she came to see the apartment her daughter had been excited about over the telephone. "I mean, why this one instead of all the other places you've seen for the past month? I don't see what it has that's so different from those others. Why did you hold out so long?"

Elizabeth couldn't explain it herself. "Maybe it's the fern, huh, Ma?" she laughed.

Elizabeth didn't know why she had taken the apartment so promptly. She began to feel that it was because she had been so exhausted that day she first saw it and that she most probably realized that time was at a premium in regard to her finding something. On the other hand, she certainly did not feel that she had made a mistake when she moved in.

"Whose fern is that?" Elizabeth asked the superintendent. On closer inspection, it was in very bad condition—the leaves had yellowed and some of them were covered with mealybugs.

"It belonged to the previous tenant, but it's mine now. I just haven't had a chance to remove it. But if you want it, you can have it, wicker basket and all—for fifteen dollars."

Comprehending the rip-off attitude of many superintendents with whom she had dealt before, Elizabeth smiled benignly and told the unshaven, gruff man (who was a perfect match for his wife) that she indeed wanted the plant. From that day on she referred to it as her good-luck fern.

Elizabeth grew to love her small apartment. She arranged her furniture so that the alcove was the dining area, the larger portion of the room becoming a combination living room and bedroom. She had purchased a large convertible couch which was placed facing the picture window.

Elizabeth loved music and bought an exceptionally good stereo system the week after moving in.

"You couldn't wait?" her mother exclaimed. "You know you are almost broke from this move and yet you had to go out and get such expensive equipment—and on credit no less. I thought you once said that you would never buy anything on credit?"

"I had to have it, Mom." Elizabeth explained. "My old machine isn't working anymore, and you know how I love to hear my records. I haven't been going out at all. I even take my lunch to work. I felt it was necessary, it helps me relax."

Elizabeth had an extensive collection of semiclassical music, mostly operettas and Broadway musicals. On her way home from work at the end of her second week in her new home, she went to a record store with the intention of buying some new albums. Classical music was definitely not to her taste, but she suddenly found herself in front of the classical record display. Elizabeth stood there looking at the albums and reached out for a record, on the cover of which was a stunning photograph of a butterfly landing on a fern. The album was a recording of Mendelssohn's Concerto in E Minor, Opus 64. Elizabeth had never heard of it before. Compulsively, she took the album to the check-out counter and paid for it.

When she arrived back in her apartment, Elizabeth recalls removing the album from its package and being quite angry with herself. "Why the hell did I buy this?" she asked aloud. She felt as though she had been a victim of impulsive buying, something she disliked in others and especially in herself. A response to the packaging, the shot of the butterfly on the fern, had been so impressive that she had paid six dollars to have it without even knowing what music was contained on the recording. Angrily, she put the unopened album with her other records in the cabinet under the phonograph.

Although Elizabeth was ecstatically happy with her new apartment, there were certain times when a mood of melancholy overcame her while she was there. It was an almost wistful feeling. For hours at a time Elizabeth would sit on her sofa opposite the picture window and watch the boats as they passed on the Hudson River below. This didn't happen often, but when it did, Elizabeth would later become extremely upset about it. She was a most active person, working on various craft projects, going to dance classes, attending Broadway plays. She was always on the move.

Why do I sit there for hours on end without moving? she would contemplate. I must be getting old or something.

The fern that Elizabeth inherited, at a price, had taken on a new life due to the loving care that she heaped on it. The plant responded to her touch, and in just a few weeks after she had moved into the apartment, the fern perked up bright green, sprouting several new fronds.

On August 28, 1973, Elizabeth was at home with a case of the flu. She had been doctoring herself by getting plenty of rest, taking large doses of vitamin C, plus a liquid anticold medication. The cold remedy had made her drowsy and she fell off to sleep. About an hour later she awoke. Her cold seemed worse. She reached for the insipid green liquid and took another dose, not remembering that it had been but a very short time since she had initially ingested the foul-tasting stuff.

The effects of this overdose created hallucinations. The room spun and she kept nodding off and awakening every few minutes. She felt as though she was in an uncontrollable drunken stupor. Finally, she went into a deep sleep and had a most horrendous nightmare.

The bad dream started out with Elizabeth on a boat, some sort of a huge yacht. She didn't know where it was headed nor whose boat it was. There were other people on board the vessel, and after a time she began to realize that many of them were friends that she had in her waking life.

In this nightmare, Elizabeth recalled that a man who was a stranger to her suddenly appeared and smiled. She responded in like manner. Later, she couldn't help but remember that he had a face much like that of her "ideal man," Rock Hudson. In the dream the man proceeded to act in a most polite, mild-mannered fashion toward Elizabeth. He asked the waiter to bring some drinks and he held the chair away from the table as Elizabeth sat down. Elizabeth said that she recalled talking with the man in her dream for what seemed like hours. Although she couldn't remember any of the specifics regarding the conversation, she knows that the time was a happy, peaceful one.

Toward the end of the dream, the man suddenly clasped both arms around himself, emitting a piercing scream. He ran to the railing of the boat and held onto it. The ocean had become rough and waves lashed at the vessel. In a sudden lurch, the man was flung overboard into the pounding waves.

At this point, Elizabeth said that her dream became most lifelike. She attempted to reach out for the man but he kept going under. Elizabeth watched in abject terror as the man drowned in front of her. She then awoke from the dream with a start, soaked in perspiration. For the rest of the night Elizabeth sat staring blankly out of the window. She cried the entire time.

"Someday, someday my dumb little daughter,

you're going to kill yourself taking all that damn medicine the way you do." Elizabeth's mother was most upset when the story was related to her. "You should throw it out, that medicine, all of it in fact—aspirins and all. You rely on that stuff too much."

As time passed, Elizabeth fell into the mood of melancholic cogitation more frequently. Although she didn't want these periods of vague wistfulness, on some other level of consciousness she felt twinges of anticipation for them. She became aware of the submerged anticipatory aspects of her dilemma. That upset her to the point of deciding to consult with a psychiatrist. A friend who lived in New York City recommended her own psychiatrist, Dr. Sidney R——. The psychiatrist attempted to uncover the reason for her bouts with the anticipated depression but had little success.

Dr. R.: Are you always depressed, Elizabeth?

Elizabeth: Not always, no . . . only at certain times. Maybe three or four times a month now; it has increased.

Dr. R.: Where do you have these states of depression, at home, at your office, in the street?

Elizabeth: Only at home in my apartment. But I love my apartment.

Dr. R.: How long does the depression last?

Elizabeth: About four to eight hours. But I really don't know if it can be truthfully described as a state of depression. It's more like a kind of nostalgia, a sadness that's—well, almost enjoyable. And I am completely relaxed while this is happening. I almost like it, and that's what bothers me. By nature I'm an up person. I enjoy life. I shy away from any kind of sadness. I won't attend funerals, even those in my immediate family. In this particular instance, I seem to have no choice in the matter. I almost look forward to these sad occasions.

Dr. R.: You say you look forward to them, these periods of depression, that you almost enjoy them in some way. What do you mean by this?

Elizabeth: Well, it's rather a comfortable feeling, I mean I feel comfortable while it is occurring. Although I realize that it is not constructive and that I am wasting time, and that sitting on the sofa for hours at a time is a downer, I can't help myself. I just sit there, almost on the verge of crying, and for what reason I cannot say. It's like a loss of something or someone, but I don't know what or who. I haven't lost anything or anyone to feel this way. I just sit there, frozen, unable to move.

Dr. R.: What goes on in your mind when you are in one of these states?

Elizabeth: Nothing in particular. I just concentrate on the boats below. Or else I watch the lights over in Manhattan come on if it's dusk. Or, I simply stare up at the sky.

Dr. R.: But tell me why this upsets you so, why this worries you?

Elizabeth: Because its not natural . . . I mean for *me* it isn't. And it's almost as though I were watching myself get into this state, and I'm quite helpless to get out of it. Also, there is this dream I have been having recently, several times. I've never had a bad dream before.

Elizabeth then told the doctor her nightmare about the man on the boat. She had had the nightmare on four subsequent occasions.

Dr. R: Maybe this is just a fear because you do not currently have a man in your life. The man in the dream seems to be molded in the image of your ideal man. In your description of the man in the dream you have described the same man—physically as well as character wise—that you, in reality, wish to meet. He is charming, polite, the man of your desires. You carry on a conversation with him for what seems like many hours. He seems to be intelligent. He is, in fact, everything you desire in a man. His drowning, I believe, stems from an unconscious fear that you will not be able to have such a man in your life, or, that if you did find him you might lose him.

The psychiatrist's response to her dilemma seemed scientifically sound, but deep within herself Elizabeth felt that there had to be more to the dream than that. She did not have a deep yearning to be married, nor did she feel that being over thirty years of age meant that she might "miss the boat" in regard to getting a man. (Dr. R. felt the boat in Elizabeth's dream represented life itself.)

Several weeks passed. Elizabeth's mother was now very much concerned over her daughter's irrational behavior. She suggested that Elizabeth move out of the apartment and find another: "After all, you began to have these problems when you moved in here."

"No, Mother!" Elizabeth defended her home. "I love this apartment. I'm not going to give it up."

One rainy Saturday afternoon, Elizabeth got up late and made brunch for herself. She began to play some of her records. Browsing through her albums, she came to the record with the butterfly and the fern on its jacket cover. It was the Mendelssohn concerto that she had purchased so compulsively. She removed the record from its sleeve and placed it on the turntable. I might as well hear what this sounds like, she thought. She then went over to the sofa and began reading one of the novels she hadn't had time to start before.

After a few moments, Elizabeth found herself putting down the book and listening to the music. The violins in the Mendelssohn piece were indeed lovely, and a thought crossed her mind that she might be more tolerant of classical music.

As the record played, Elizabeth watched the rain-swept river below; the smoke of several passing ships mingled with the heavy mist created an eerie, unreal panorama. Elizabeth was soon overwhelmed by the romantic mood cast by the concerto.

When the record was through playing, Elizabeth went over to the machine and started the concerto from the beginning again. This time she turned the volume up quite loud. The music filled her small apartment with its contrasting crescendos and diminuendos. Tears came to Elizabeth's eyes as a feeling of complete, utter loss overtook her.

Again the record ended. Again Elizabeth started it from the beginning. She did this five or six times.

The sound of the front door chimes jarred her from what was an almost trancelike state. It was her next-door neighbor, Sheila Robbins. The woman stood in the doorway, ashen-faced, hands trembling.

"What's the matter?" Elizabeth asked.

"It's that music. . . ."

"Oh, I'm sorry," Elizabeth apologized, interrupting her neighbor before the woman could finish her sentence. "I guess it's too loud. I'll turn it down."

"No," Mrs. Robbins stated. "It's not too loud. That doesn't bother me. It isn't that it's loud . . . it's, oh, it's probably just a coincidence."

"What's a coincidence?" Elizabeth asked.

"Well . . . I . . ." the woman stammered, staring into the apartment.

"Look, why don't you come in?" Elizabeth invited her perturbed neighbor into the apartment. "I'll make a cup of coffee. I could use the company myself."

Sheila Robbins stepped into Elizabeth Towland's apartment hesitantly. In a few moments coffee was brewing and Elizabeth offered her neighbor cookies.

"What's the problem?" Elizabeth again asked Mrs. Robbins.

"Well, it's really silly, I guess," the blond fortyish woman tried to explain. "Do you know anything about the man who lived here before you?" Mrs. Robbins asked.

"Well," Elizabeth answered, "not exactly. The nosy superintendent's wife told me the apartment had become available only because he had died. She made it sound as though the apartments in the building were so desirable that people only left in case of tragedy. I brushed that off as her sales pitch."

"Well, he did die," Mrs. Robbins said.

"Not here in the apartment?" Elizabeth exclaimed. Why else would the woman be so unable to verbalize what was bothering her?

"No," Mrs. Robbins said. "He died in the hospital. But he had been very ill here in the apartment for quite some time before he went into the hospital."

"What was the matter with him?" Elizabeth asked.

"He had advanced emphysema. Poor guy, he'd cough for hours. Could hear him all the way down the hall. And he was so apologetic about it whenever you'd meet him, in the lobby or down in the laundry room. The cough got worse and went into pneumonia. They took him to the hospital by ambulance. He died a few days later. They found him one morning literally choked to death on his own fluids. They said it was just like drowning."

"And what about the music?" Elizabeth asked.

"Well, he loved the classics. Especially anything by Mendelssohn. That's all he would do toward the end, just play his records. When I heard that record

24

you were playing today, it really made my hair stand on end. That was one of the Mendelssohn pieces he would play. It was like some dumb TV show, you know, where the dead man comes back, his ghost plays the music he liked, and all that kind of weird thing."

Elizabeth, now much disturbed, asked her neighbor what the man's name had been."

"Mark . . . Mark Saunders. He was really quite a nice person. He knew that I was home during the day and would always apologize to me about playing the music, would even call me on the phone to ask if he might play it louder than usual sometimes. I told him sure. I knew he was really sick. Would cough all through the night sometimes."

"About how old was he?" Elizabeth asked.

"That was the tragedy. He was only thirty-seven or thirty-eight. He was really a terrific neighbor before he became sick. He was a lawyer, always helpful. A lot of people came to him for advice about their rents which had been boosted, which they felt was illegal. He always helped them out, too . . . free of charge. When he had a party, he'd always invite us and some of the other neighbors over. Was afraid that the noise would bother us, annoy us, so he felt that we should be at the party rather than listening to it through the walls. He was also a happy man. I really liked him, miss him a lot around here."

By this time Elizabeth was completely distracted and wanted to be alone. She excused herself saying that she really wasn't feeling too well and led Mrs.

Robbins to the door. On the way out of Elizabeth's apartment, Mrs. Robbins stopped when she spotted the fern."

"Oh, you have Mark's fern. It certainly has gotten quite large. It was one of his favorite plants. He loved growing things . . . had them in the window, even hanging from the ceiling. I'd tell him that I couldn't grow a thing, that every plant I had would eventually die off. He told me that I had to give my growing things some love, talk to them. He had several books about that kind of thing. Do you believe in that? That plants can respond to one's thoughts? Well, anyway, how come his family left that fern? They managed to clean everything else out within two days after he died."

"It was almost dead," Elizabeth explained. "I guess they didn't think that it was worth transporting."

Mrs. Robbins turned in the doorway and glanced over to the window, where rain was trickling down the pane. "He really suffered before they took him to the hospital, poor guy. He'd just sit and stare out that window, playing that Mendelssohn. He'd tell me that he had been sitting for ten hours at a time, just staring out the window. I didn't know whether to believe him or not, I mean, ten hours! But he really wanted to be alone those last weeks. I think he knew he was not going to get well, that he might die. Maybe that's why he spent so much time looking out the window. He told me that he used to read a lot, but toward the end he didn't have the patience even for that."

Elizabeth's line of thought was one-directional as she asked her neighbor another question. "What did he look like?"

"Mark?" Mrs. Robbins replied. "Oh, tall, darkish, kind of an all-American type. Not to my own personal taste, you understand, but you could say that he was a handsome man. And what a personality—always a gentleman, considerate. He was most upset about the woman's movement, but for an odd reason. He felt that he wouldn't be able to treat women the way he liked if they lost some of their, and I quote him, 'femininity.' He loved to hold the door for you, stand up when you came into the room, you know, that kind of thing. Old-fashioned as heck, but with him you really felt like he meant it—it wasn't just the thing to do because it was proper."

"Could . . . would you say that he looked like Rock Hudson in any way?" Elizabeth asked, almost afraid to hear the answer.

"Well, stretching the imagination a bit you could say that. He did have the stature, tall, and the complexion and those almost perfect features. I often felt that he should have been a movie actor instead of a lawyer. I guess you could say that he was a Rock Hudson type, if anything.

"Well," Mrs. Robbins continued when she didn't get any further response from Elizabeth. "I've got a hairdresser appointment this afternoon, got to hurry along. You know you really put a scare into me for a moment with that music. Aren't coincidences strange?"

Elizabeth closed the door behind Mrs. Robbins. She had tried not to show it, but she had been shaken to the very depths of her being when she had learned about Mark Saunders. She was frightened. There was no other possible explanation for her recent behavior. In some way the man who had lived in that apartment before her had reached out to her. Why else had she purchased the Mendelssohn record? How else could she explain why she spent countless hours sitting at the window, feeling sad, nostalgic, and unable to move? And, most important, was it not an acceptable explanation for her dream? The man she had seen in her nightmare could easily have been Mark Saunders.

Elizabeth wasn't a believer in the supernatural, but she had some friends who were. Elizabeth invited them over to her apartment the following weekend. She told them the story. It was suggested that Elizabeth get in touch with a psychic or a "ghost chaser." One of them knew of my work in the field of parapsychology and recommended that Elizabeth contact me.

I told Elizabeth Towland that I would rather visit her apartment for our meeting. The next week I crossed the George Washington Bridge, found the building where Elizabeth lived, and rang her doorbell. She let me in and we sat on the sofa.

The view was indeed extremely beautiful. It was not difficult to discern strong vibrations in the room. These vibrations were not Elizabeth's. There was a heaviness, an odd calm, a feeling that something other than the two of us was in the apartment.

Because Elizabeth had a lack of knowledge in matters pertaining to the occult, it was difficult for me to convince her that Mark Saunders' vibrations had been so strong in life that they had somehow remained in the apartment. Elizabeth had been able to subconsciously pick up Mark's vibrations from the apartment in the manner that a psychometrist does with a piece of jewelry or an article of clothing. His vibrations had become so pronounced that they had begun to influence Elizabeth. She had been utilized as some form of medium by Mark's continuing vibrations and was duly influenced by them at certain times when her own telepathic and extra-communicative energy levels were high.

"I don't really believe in ghosts," Elizabeth declared.

I told her that it wasn't necessarily a ghost or a complete entity. The energy that the man created, his vibrations, remained in the last place where he had spent so much time on earth. There was evidence that he had heard about and possibly studied the occult: Mrs. Robbins announced that Mark Saunders did read books on ESP, communication with plants, and other paranormal topics. It was also conceivable that the ill man spent some of his time meditating, building up his physical energy through the power of the mind. Possibly, he had even done psychic healing on himself. With this kind of influence it was no wonder that the apartment retained some of the man's psychic energy.

"But I'm not interested in anything like that," Elizabeth proclaimed a bit disdainfully. "If what you say is true, why would the vibrations of this man try to get through to *me*? And why would I instantly fall in love with a place where the vibrations, or whatever, were going to be harmful? This *is* all very negative, at least to my way of thinking."

"Well," I reasoned, "Mark Saunders was physically and mentally exactly like the kind of man you wished to meet. Unconsciously, you picked this up the very first time that you entered this apartment."

Elizabeth listened intently as I continued. "You had found your man, at least his vibrations. You kept saying to everyone that you experienced a feeling of loss when you went into the states of depression. I feel that this was due to the loss of a man who no longer existed on a physical level. But your subconscious was tuned in to the man's vibratory level. In some way, Mark Saunders was still very much evident. When you would fall off to sleep, especially in a deep subconscious dream state—as in the time you overdosed on the cold remedy—Mark Saunders' physical self was even made apparent to you. It is like a good psychometrist—who is usually able to describe the person who owned whatever article is being psychometrized. You even picked up on the cause of Mark's death when you dreamed of his drowning. This also represented to you that in this life you could not get together with him, that he was no longer here. Thus the feeling of loss."

"What about the music?" Elizabeth asked.

"Well, on the subconscious level, you were completely aware of Mark Saunders. I believe that some of his likes and dislikes were somehow solidified through your own subconscious. You somehow carried his vibrations with you, though subconsciously. When you purchased the Mendelssohn recording, it was for Mark Saunders and not yourself. Do you think that all this can be coincidental? You told me that this beige color on the walls that Mark Saunders left behind was your favorite color, that you loved plants and especially ferns. So many seemingly insignificant things that in truth hold great significance."

"This really does sound like something out of *Night Gallery*, or some other TV show," Elizabeth adamantly stated. "I really don't know if I can put any credence in it. Why would I have to go through this? It was an almost torturous experience, after all. If it's true, then what possible good does it all do? What does it all mean, at least to me?"

"I don't believe in coincidence," I proceeded with my psychic explanation. "This entire happening was not accidental. I believe that karma is involved. There was a lesson here for you, and that is that you are not meant to live with the aura of an ideal man hovering over your life. He doesn't really exist, at least for you. And if you were to find such a man, you most probably would lose him, for one reason or another. I believe that you were attracted to this place because of Mark Saunders' vibrations, but your coming here and taking the apartment was not chance. You were meant to have this experience. But it is time to release your thoughts of a dream man. You are meant to move into a more realistic state, and this is forcing you to do it. I believe that every psychic experience relates directly to the person having it, and that important lessons are to be gleaned from such experiences. Psychic phenomena do not exist without justifiable cause and effect; the person having such an experience must recognize it as such."

"I don't know if I can go along with that rationalization," Elizabeth said, straight out. "But it's something to think about."

Several months later, our mutual friends informed me that Elizabeth had decided to move out of the apartment. When she did, she had begun dating men not like her idealized, romanticized man. She appeared to be more happy than before and was even talking to her friends about a possible marital situation.

"Does Elizabeth ever have any more of these states of depression?" I asked her friends.

"No," one of them replied. "She hasn't had any such experience since moving out of that strange apartment. And she seems to think it will not ever be repeated. She says that after a few more repeats of the dream and the depressed mood she got into, she finally decided that it possibly *could* be the apartment. She doesn't admit to believing that the ghost or whatever of that guy was in some way getting to her, but we feel that this could be a realization on her part.

Anyway, what matters is that it hasn't occurred since her move; she is free from it. And she certainly has changed."

Elizabeth has progressed on several levels of awareness because of her experience in the apartment. If not me, then someone else would have come into her awareness to somehow enlighten her. She had been cutting herself off from new experiences by keeping her standard of a dream man, and the time was right for her to experience other things. Whether Elizabeth believed it was the vibrations of Mark Saunders or not, the experience motivated her to try a different mode of living. And, very possibly, Mark Saunders had some kind of karmic pattern that *he* had to work out by being made a part of Elizabeth's experiences. I have not been back to Elizabeth's apartment in New Jersey, but I often wonder if the new tenant after Elizabeth has had any experiences with the vibrations of Mark Saunders.

2

"The Physical Emanations of Life"

At this point I think that it is important to define the word "vibrations" so that we can reach an understanding of what they are. There are so many definitions, but different interpretations all reach the same conclusion.

Here and throughout this book, I'll quote from a direct transcript of a group interview I had with several persons of diverse backgrounds. Each of them had different religious histories, but all were presently involved in one form or another of mind expansion or spiritual awareness. They will be referred to by initial; names and gender are unimportant to the conclusive summation.

October 6, 1974. New York

D. Logan (*addressing group*): This is a free open approach; therefore, say whatever you wish; feel free to express yourselves in any way, okay? The name of the book I am doing is *Vibrations*, and each of you in this group has had at least some development in the area of awareness. I would like you to tell me in your own words what the term "vibrations" means to you.

E. (age fifty-two): I don't know the technical, scientific term, but I do think that we are each made up of energies of some kind, forms of electricity, and these energies in us change at times and other people can pick that up, and sense the changed energies.

V. (age thirty-eight): Vibrations are to me the physical emanations of light and life. All living things have vibrations. Anything made of matter has vibratory emanations. And in the psychic sense, vibrations mean *feelings*. When I hold a person's ring, I get feelings from it—sometimes something of the past or even the future. Also, his personality, and of those relationships around him. It's an inner knowing.

Once I held an object of art from the Orient. In my mind's eye there immediately sprung a vision of some kind—a Chinese fishing junk, fields of rice paddies, huts of straw. I could even "see" people working in the fields. It was a bit frightening but exciting, it was very real.

V. was talking about the psychometry of objects, the method in which the vibrations from a piece of jewelry, an article of clothing, a photograph, anything in fact, are transmitted to one holding or touching any of those objects. Psychometry can be done on people and places as well as on objects.

Logan: When or how do you get these feelings?

V.: Sometimes in a store I will be standing next to a person and I will tune in to his vibrations and become upset. I will want to get away from that person as soon as I can. Sometimes I will even know *why* I feel that way. Sometimes it's a nervous high-strung energy and I just will not want to be near that person.

Logan: Do you get vibrations from any kind of people?

V.: Many times I meet people and respond to them instantly—there's a feeling of familiarity.

E.: Vibrations are a physical thing, well almost a physical thing. Sometimes it is something you can almost touch, that's what I mean by physical. I sort of feel vibrations like electricity going through a room.

Logan: You said "going through a room." Do you mean any room, maybe a room you haven't been in before?

E.: Oh, yes . . . you can definitely sense them that way too. You can feel an up, or positive, vibration or a negative, down vibration—at least I can.

Logan: What about the electricity you speak of?

E.: Well, when I'm meditating, I can feel the vibrations in the room start to build. It's almost a kind of sound, a crackling, the kind you get in electricity. They make you feel good, physically as well as mentally. You know, it's also like when you meet someone for the first time and you say they have good vibes or bad vibes. You can sense it coming from them. It's in the atmosphere.

Ralph was ten when I first met him in 1965. He is the son of a well-known actress and had been brought up in the world of awareness through his mother's interest in the occult and psychic phenomena. Ralph's mother had sought me out to give her son a psychic reading. At that initial meeting, I noted that Ralph's energy level was quite high, his aura appeared to me a bright blue-green with a ridge of gold on the outside. Ralph didn't know what he wanted to be when he grew up, but expressed the hope that it would entail positive, constructive expression.

As he went through his early school years, Ralph didn't openly express the thoughts and ideas that his mother had afforded him. He was afraid of being tabbed a "kook" and didn't wish to appear different from his school chums. Having attended public school in New York City, I can imagine the reaction of Ralph's schoolmates if he had made public this aspect of his life. Ralph actually hid learned spiritual information from his friends, bringing true meaning to the definition of "occult." Despite this, Ralph had countless friends through his early years. They were not merely acquaintances; deep, lasting friendships evolved. He attracted friends like sweetened water does hummingbirds. You could say that he had a "following," almost like that of a TV or rock star. People befriended him, came to love him, and placed complete trust in him.

It should be stated here that Ralph is not especially good-looking; he was also not the brightest kid in his age bracket. His mind tends to wander too much for him to be a top student and his interests are not in typical subject matters. What is clear is that Ralph did not attract his countless numbers of close friends in physical or mental ways. What Ralph has is a very clearly pronounced aura, a strong vibratory level. Ralph was never ostentatious; he never asked for the kind of teen-age adulation that he received.

"Aren't you aware that you have a huge number of close friends, more than I have ever seen anyone have?" I once asked him.

"I like people" was his only explanation.

Ralph would never once say or even intimate that he was anything special or that he had any secret ability. He would never even talk about it.

Ralph's vibrations did the work for him. Later,

Ralph decided to become a singer. His success is now taking place as he exudes the same vibrations onstage as he does in life. I expect to see his name emblazoned on the marquees before too long.

"What makes Ralph so special?" I'd ask one of his young friends.

"I don't know exactly" was the teen-ager's reply. "I mean, like the guy's an up person. He's cool, digs people, relates to them. You know, like a brother rather than a friend. You just want to be around him, that's all."

You just want to be around him. This to me proves the power of an aura, a positive vibratory level that can emanate from someone. Through association with positive, spiritual awareness ever since he was a child, Ralph had built a vibratory field around himself so powerful that it attracted others to him even though they did not know, nor could they verbalize, what it was that made them wish to be with him.

The theory of vibratory emanations can be traced back to the beginning of mankind. The sacred books of the Egyptians, of Hermes, and of the Orient tell us that these ancient peoples not only believed but practiced the theory of auras. Paracelsus was one of the first scientists in the West to delve into the belief of the astral body. He proved that an often visible radiation or, as he termed it, "a fiery globe" surrounded the physical body.

It wasn't until the early 1700s that science began to take an interest in the theory that vibrations and auras surrounding people do exist. Anton Mesmer, born in 1734, was a doctor who became interested in magnetism and the emanations that come from pieces of steel and magnets. He was the first scientist to anticipate the modern-day theory of an electromagnetic basis of life. Mesmer was to find that the same conditions and effects found in ferromagnetism were also induced by the emanations that flowed from the human hand. He named this vibratory force "animal magnetic fluid," more commonly known as "animal magnetism."

In Vienna, Mesmer established a clinic where he utilized magnetic healing. Unfortunately, Mesmer became infatuated with his own fame and dealt with the sensational aspects of this newfound science. Like the more sensation-seeking adherents of psychic phenomena of today, Mesmer got caught up in the theatrics, in the dramatic aspects of his work. He held what were called "magnetic séances"; these were usually evenings that bordered on hysteria by his often fanatical followers. A scientific commission set up to examine animal magnetism stated that it could "find no proof of the existence of the animal magnetic fluid that Mesmer says he has discovered." Since that time, many scientists have said that if Mesmer had indeed not known how to correctly demonstrate scientifically an aura or vibrations that emanated from the human constitution, then the commissioners should themselves have made proper investigations. They did not.

Mesmer fell into disrepute and died in virtual

obscurity. The theory of animal magnetism, openly condemned by science, was not researched for many years because of the adverse publicity. However, there were some scientists who did believe in the theory or a form of it and worked on it undercover, privately. In 1845 Baron Karl von Reichenbach claimed to have discovered that there was a radiation that emanated from certain objects. He named this the "odic force." Von Reichenbach said that this force could be seen with the naked eye and was generated not only by magnets and crystals but by the human body as well. Von Reichenbach worked in a very objective manner. He would have mediumistic types sit in darkened rooms. Many of the mediums were able to perceive flames of sparks, light rays, or sometimes fiery colors coming from magnets placed in front of them. The light rays exuded were of different colors and could be seen emanating not only from the magnets but from crystals and plant life as well.

Finally, Von Reichenbach brought in live subjects and placed them, unclothed, in front of the mediums in the darkened rooms. The mediums said that they were able to "see" rays of light emanating from the human hand, the fingertips to be exact. Later this "odylic cloud" was successfully photographed.

In 1920, Dr. W. J. Kilner wrote his book *Human Atmosphere* (George Routledge and Sons, Ltd.). It was much ahead of its time. Kilner had been medical electrician at St. Thomas Hospital in London. In his book Kilner told of his scientific method of observing auras. Kilner had done his work with the assumption that the vibrations emanating from people were actually ultraviolet rays of some sort. Usually, under normal circumstances, ultraviolet lights cannot be seen by the human eye as their vibratory rate is much too high for ordinary vision. Apparently, the aura could not be seen unassisted except by extremely sensitive persons. Therefore, Kilner worked on creating something that could screen out the light rays, leaving only the ultraviolet rays to be viewed. His screen was a cell of optically ground glass that had been shaped like an excessively narrow box. The box contained an alcoholic solution of decyanin, which is a coal tar dye.

An observer in the Kilner experiments would get himself ready to view an aura by first looking through the screen at some very bright light, such as a hundred-watt bulb. Before the light emanating through the decyanin wears off, the observer casts his gaze at a human subject, usually undressed, who has been placed against a black background in the darkened room. Kilner discovered that every human being had an aura, a faint, almost colorous glow that extended away from the body up to two feet. The entire body was outlined in this glow, which was somewhat oval in shape.

As the same subject was viewed through this screen over a period of time, sometimes several weeks, it was found that the emanations varied in clarity and size. If the subject was feeling well on a given day, the aura would be vibrant and extend out quite far. If the subject was ill or had any mental problem, the aura contracted and became almost undetectable.

Kilner devised methods of diagnosing disease through his study of the aura. Specific diseases, such as epilepsy and hysteria, were indicated in the aura by certain changes common to a particular illness. He also found that women were able to produce changes in their aura almost at will, with but the slightest effort.

What Kilner was seeing were the vibrations of the "etheric body." When healthy, the human body emanates a vital force or an energy field that has been stored up. This can be seen radiating in straight lines outward from the body, in all directions. When the subject is ill, the etheric body becomes attenuated and is not able to expel this force.

Kilner also found that extremely positive auras could activate auras that were weak due to illness or negative mental attitudes. In like manner, an extremely weak aura would draw upon those that were stronger. The comparison to the recharging of batteries is quite apt.

Slowly, work was done in the field of aura or vibration reading, but the scientific approach in the United States left much to be desired. It wasn't until the middle 1960s, when the book *Psychic Discoveries Behind the Iron Curtain* became an international best seller, that interest once again focused on scientific aura research in the U.S.S.R., where Semyon and

Valentina Kirlian have devoted their entire lives to the development of their very extraordinary kind of electrical photography. It was the Kirlians who proved beyond a doubt that energy fields do exist in and around organic as well as inorganic materials.

The Kirlian photographs of the Russian healer Krivorotov proved the existence of healing vibrations. When Krivorotov was in a state of rest, Kirlian photography of his thumb (magnified five hundred times) revealed a completely different energy field than when he was healing, when the emanations from the thumb become increased in size, intensity, and number. Finally, science in America has become interested enough to utilize a form of vibration photography. Although it is quite early for the results to be tabulated, there have been some very positive experiments with the American form of this kind of photography.

During the years that I held psychic development classes as a trance medium, much data pertaining to vibrations, and their cause and effect upon the individual, was brought through by Dr. Stanley, the consciousness that works through me. The following was culled from a trance session held at that time. The question was put forth by a student of mine.

Question: Having been a scientist in your most recent incarnation, we would like to know your feelings on psychic vibrations that we are told emanate from us. Can you afford us some enlightenment?

Dr. Stanley: Everything that exists is made up of vibrations . . . the smallest cell can be broken down into an energy or vibratory form, imperceptible to even the most astute of scientific inventions. This energy is the basis of every living thing, everything that has ever been alive in some form . . . it is the energy of all creation. The energy is the same; the grouping of the cells brings about the different and various forms of life. This energy is what is now being sensed in your Kirlian photography. It does change in sickness and health, in mental and spiritual attitudes. Also, the colors that can be perceived in individual auras do indeed signify the mental and spiritual as well as the physical state of being.

R. (age twenty-eight): Vibrations to me are very definite sense feelings that I receive about places and persons. I have had these feelings, this ability to feel things about others, since I was a child. I discovered that the bad vibrations I pick up on some people is not my own insecurity, but rather their own insecurities they were unconsciously throwing off and I was receiving. I had not even taken this into account before. When I began to become more aware of myself, I discovered it *was* the other person I was picking up something negative about.

Logan: In other words, when you met someone for the first time and get bad vibes from them, you immediately felt that there was something wrong with yourself and not the other person, but now you realize that you were indeed unconsciously psyching out the other party?

R.: Exactly. In many instances, the bad vibes do indeed come from them. An interesting thing happened to me recently. I had mentioned to someone else that I had received very bad vibrations from this one particular person that we both had met. I felt that it was *my* hang-up, *my* own insecurity in this instance. This friend I said this to told me it was funny I had said that, for many people get this very same reaction from this person; each said that it most probably was his or her own insecurity. Those who were picking up something from this particular person's vibrations thought something was wrong with *themselves*. I feel in many instances that your own vibrations could change another person's, if you affect him in a negative way. For example, there might be something in your physical makeup or something that you might say that would cause negative vibrations to be sent out by the one that you are meeting. It isn't always the other person. You might bring out the negative vibrations in them.

Logan: Do you make use of vibrations in your own life?

R.: I haven't developed them, they just sort of are there despite myself. I mean, it's nothing I actively do. I pick up these vibrations in rooms or persons.

N. (age forty-one): Vibrations to me are a quality of feeling, my capacity to be aware, to respond. When I walk into a room, I'm trying to sense the feelings that are in that room.

Logan: Do you mean that you consciously try to pick up vibrations when you enter a room?

N.: I have discovered that I do . . . this is what my

whole self-awareness is keyed to. And when I walk into a strange room there is an overall feeling at first, and then as I begin to talk to people or merely watch them, I am aware of specific vibrations that come from them . . . I pick up different qualities of feelings.

Logan: This is something you learned?

N.: I'm saying that I have found that I have been doing this unconsciously, and now that I have become aware of it, I cooperate with it more.

Logan: Have you ever let it influence you? If you were to enter a strange room and were introduced to someone and you felt some bad vibes emanating from that person, well, what would you do?

N.: I'd wait and see. I wouldn't be as likely to attempt to make contact with that person. I would try to feel out why I felt that way, what it was that I picked up from that person's vibrations.

Logan: And what about later? When you do make actual contact with the person that you got the bad vibes from. Are your initial feelings about the person's vibrations proven to be correct most of the time?

N.: If I stay in touch with that awareness, yes. For instance, I say that I discovered this awareness. I discovered that this is going on all the time and that I am unconsciously affected. When I became more aware of myself, I was able to deal with it a little more adequately. For instance, if I feel that someone I met is giving off negative vibrations, I would tell myself that I must be nice to this stranger and then go over and talk with them. Then I usually discover that I am very tense and somehow really unable to relate to that person. I find myself responding to what I at first sensed as bad vibrations. My good intentions of going over to the person I received bad vibes on would fail.

Logan: Have you ever come across someone that you were attracted to, that you felt had good vibrations, and that you might later on discover that the person had been faking those initial vibrations?

N.: This is an interesting question because it happens to deal with my own level of awareness. I have certainly made that mistake, many times. I found that before I was in touch with what I was *truly* picking up, I would psyche myself to like the person in question, go out of my way to like the person. It was all mental or social impressions. I feel that my first impressions are much more reliable now that I am aware of what I am actually sensing, what I am picking up—without preprogramming it, without precoloring it by anticipating. And my own awareness-searching has opened this up for me.

For instance, you go to a lecture to hear someone speak about a certain subject that you are interested in. Naturally, you are already predisposed to like that person; you assume that you are going to have something in common with the lecturer. It is a form of preprogramming. And I was often fooled by this. Just because the person is speaking about a subject matter you are also interested in doesn't mean that you will like that person. When I just do nothing in my head, when I do not conceive of either liking or disliking a person I meet for the first time, if I'm just there and in touch with my own awareness, I do not make the kind of mistake of being fooled frequently. Not always, but quite often I find that there is a kind of basic perception, a picking up, or responding to vibrations that come from others which I can trust now, if I just let it happen.

Your true vibratory level cannot be hidden or covered up in any physical way. It shows through and is consciously or unconsciously sensed by others. A classic example of this was the actress Marilyn Monroe, whom I had met twice.

Marilyn Monroe was an extremely deep, ever searching, horrifyingly honest person. Her shocking childhood was responsible for her acute sensitivity. She became the victim of producers who stuck her in tightly fitted clothes, smeared gross makeup on her face, dyed her hair an unbelievable platinum blond, and gave her whorelike parts to play on the screen. They hoped to disguise the true sensitive person Marilyn was by making her hard in appearance. But the public wasn't fooled; not for long. Despite the physical appearance that she was made to portray, the real vibrations of Marilyn Monroe showed through brightly.

Years after her death a cult has arisen around her name. Her sensitivity, her gentleness, and her ability to love are now viewed by a younger generation who see through all the gross physical nonsense inherent in most of the roles she played.

Marilyn Monroe was a bigger star in Japan than in any other country, her own included. There hasn't been a time during her life or afterward that Marilyn Monroe movies were not being shown successfully in Japan. Even today they still line up for festivals of her films. The astute Japanese, with their culture steeped in spirituality, were able to recognize Marilyn Monroe for what she in truth was, rather than the cheap, tramplike character she was usually forced to play.

My Japanese friends have always told me that it was Marilyn Monroe's "glow" that attracted them to her. "She is a lovely, sad, very human person," a Japanese once told me. "The women in my country like her even more than the men! They see in her the qualities of compassion and love that they themselves would like to express openly, but like Monroe, they have had to submerge their true feelings—she for the screen, they because of their role in Japanese society."

It is a credit to America's younger generation who are able to see and accept Monroe for what she was. I believe that it is a kind of proof that we have spiritually grown as a nation. Monroe's ludicrous attempts at portraying a sexpot are often laughed at by these young audiences. (When I was a teen-ager, Marilyn Monroe was worshiped by my contemporaries who believed she was the most fantastically sexual person who had ever lived!) Younger filmgoers see her sexual image as ridiculous, her physical attributes as lurid, but they sense the real vibrations that she emitted beneath the outward physical appearance. Her aura was not changed, altered, or destroyed. The kind, aware, sensitive person that she was is there for all to see beneath those breathy, breasty, beastly characterizations.

I never saw Marilyn Monroe in the same way that my teen-age friends did. While they whooped and hollered every time Monroe would wiggle across the screen, I would cringe in my seat. I saw only an unloved, deeply searching, extremely fragile woman, and was touched by what I sensed rather than motivated by the outlandish physicality she so amply demonstrated. Little did I then know that this is what I would later be doing professionally as an adult—seeing or sensing beyond the physical evidence at hand when giving psychic consultations and picking up on a person's true vibrations.

K. (age twenty-three): I think that you have to divide the meaning of vibrations into two distinct categories. One is the vibrations you receive from a person that is of a karmic nature. You subconsciously pick up from them something from a past life. And then I also think that there is the frequency level of vibrations. Everyone defines vibrations in their own way, and I believe that it's deep feelings that emanate from a person. And I believe these emanations are some form of electricity. If someone is very materialistic, that person will have a different vibration level than someone more spiritual. I believe certain people emanate a vibration level that only certain others can pick up on at specific times. If a person is up, aware, and "with it," this will be picked up by someone who can receive those vibrations, who is on the same vibratory level at that time.

Logan: Are you saying that we are transmitters and receivers of some kind?

K.: Exactly. If you have a certain circuit closed at a specific time, you will not react to a certain person one way or the other. This might be good, because one meets so many people today that it might be confusing if we were constantly picking up and sending out vibrations. . . . We could get overloaded, short-circuited.

A. was the youngest in the group. I stress this only because vibrations to the younger generation mean something entirely different from those in older generations.

A. (age twenty-one): Vibrations are something I take for granted. They are there, no question. I don't notice them, am not consciously aware of them. There are a lot of different things I can feed into any kind of situation: your feelings about a particular room; the group of people in a room. I do feel that everyone can pick up on negative vibes from another person.

E.: How often do you come into the presence of someone you know and immediately, even before speaking to that person, feel that something is wrong? You ask them, "What's the matter?" You sense it from them. Their vibrations are down or negative, and you immediately feel it.

Logan: Do you mean that another person might be emanating bad vibrations and that you would feel them, sense them coming from him?

E.: I would sense that he might be depressed before telling me, yes.

Logan: Well, that could be just what you see in a physical way. If someone is distressed or in pain, his face is different.

E.: But it's more than that. I really can sense a down feeling emanating from them, or an up, positive vibration if that be the case. Even if they are strangers and I have not ever met them before. It is instantaneous, even before I look at them in a totally physical way.

Professor Ernst G. Beier, (M.A. and Ph.D. in psychology) is currently at the University of Utah in Salt Lake City. His book *The Silent Language of Psychotherapy* is a classic in the field of nonverbal communication.

Dr. Beier has stated that "vibes," or vibrations, are the feelings that a person arouses in another by unobservable means. He believes that the term "vibes" is a metaphor for the communication of an emotion.

"Vibes, in another sense," Dr. Beier recently wrote in *Psychology Today* magazine, "are more than a simple message; they're an emotional climate and like any emotional climate, particularly those evoked by first impressions, they tend to be categorized by receivers as beneficial or dangerous."

Dr. Ernst goes on to state that according to the cues that vibrations from others give off, consciously or unconsciously, to a very large extent we ourselves determine the human world around us, and that we are therefore more responsible for the reactions from other persons than we dare realize.

D.: Well, I have lived in the Orient where people actively utilize vibrations in communicating with one another. When two Japanese businessmen meet for the first time, for example, it is almost ritualistic; so much bowing, so many words, much formal introduction. But after a time, I came to realize that these overformalized, ritualistic introductions were merely a device. What the two men were actually doing was attempting to get into each other's vibratory energy level, trying to pick up immediate psychic impressions from the aura that surrounds each of us. It can be most useful. The response to others' vibrations is deeply considered in many parts of the Orient.

E.: I think that one of the most common and acknowledged forms of vibratory factors that takes place between people is the so-called chemical reaction or sexual attraction. This is very obvious, and everyone has experienced it to some degree. When two people meet for the very first time and end up going to bed with one another shortly thereafter, it's got to be vibrations. What else is it? You don't know each other, you couldn't love someone immediately. What you do have is a very strong reaction to each other on some level, and I believe that is a good example of the kind of vibrations people are continually throwing off. Sometimes this immediate response of two people getting together works, and other times it's only for that one time, but there is no doubt in my mind that the initial attraction isn't merely physical.

Logan: Well, there *have* been marriages that have lasted forty years that have been initiated on a one-night-stand sexual experience. But on the other hand, people who have known each other for a long period of time marry and then divorce in a year.

A.: Usually it depends upon where you're at, in terms of your own personal development, your own awareness. If you are going through bad times, which has happened to me, at times you feel disassociated with yourself. You end up attracted to people, or they to you, who are not good for you at all. Yet in the long run they might prove good for you if you learn from the experience, bad as well as good.

R.: I don't think a lot of people do pick up on negative vibrations from others. That's why there are so many mistakes made in business relationships or in choosing certain people to be friends or lovers. I have discovered that about ninety percent of the time, initial vibrations that I pick up from people later prove correct. When meeting someone, if I don't like that person instantly, most of the time either we have nothing in common or the relationship is hostile, negative in some way. The opposite is also true. If I like from the very first the vibrations I sense from them, I discover that we do have things in common or that we can get along with each other in some ways. If I trust this psychic response to others in myself and act on it, I'm usually much better off.

It seemed to me that they all believed in the theory that each of us does indeed have vibrations—or some kind of energy field around us—and that we react off of this energy as do many who come into contact with us. But what use can it be in our daily living?

3

Your Home May Have a Message for You

Although the situation of Elizabeth Towland and her overshadowed apartment is a most dramatic one, this kind of psychic attraction to places is certainly not rare. It is no coincidence that many of the so-called ghost stories we hear about concern people who are attracted to specific areas or houses for one reason or another. Then, when the phenomena commence, either they are motivated into some change or they have some enlightenment in their lives.

Vita Girogi is a working artist who lives in lower Manhattan SoHo district—a former light industrial area that in recent years has become New York City's most active artist colony. Many available lofts that used to house small industries and concerns have attracted artists who need the space for their work. Sicilian-born, youthful, and quite dynamic, Ms. Girogi is an accomplished artist, having had several very successful showings in New York.

In 1973 Vita was standing by the front window of her apartment, deep in thought about some problem or another when she became aware of something in front of a building across the street. Vita did not know what it was that she had seen so fleetingly, but she began thinking about it. She went to her canvas, whereupon she painted three different poses of the same image. The paintings were of a flaxen-haired woman dressed in white and floating ghostlike against the facade of that building across the street. The paintings were so startingly good that the manager of her gallery was duly impressed with the work and scheduled them for an immediate showing.

Several months later, acquaintances informed Vita of a story that had been circulating around the district. An old stream had been rediscovered flowing in the basement of number 134 Spring Street. A tenant in that building, Allen Daugherty, had informed many of his friends that on countless occasions he had seen an apparition of a woman. The ghostlike emanation, he said, would hover over his bed. One day, Daugherty happened upon the SoHo Cast Iron Historic District Designation Report, which had been created to have many of the old buildings in the area designated as historical sites to keep them from being torn down.

In the report, Daugherty discovered the strange case of Juliana Elmore Sands. On January 2, 1800, Juliana was found at the bottom of the Spring Street well, which at that time had been used for drinking water. Her death became a celebrated mystery of the era. Was Juliana Sands pushed? Did she fall? Over the years there have been accounts of her ghostly appearance in the area.

The old well had been located somewhere between West Broadway and Spring Street, the same location of the building that was now directly over the stream. It was the same building in front of which Vita Girogi had first seen the flaxen-haired "ghost."

Vita became intrigued and checked old newspapers of other sightings and found that all the descriptions of the "ghost" fit the woman she had been painting. More of a coincidence was the fact that in one painting, done before her discovering anything about the "ghost," Vita had painted the spirit against the background of a cellar with many water pipes.

Vita feels that the presence is benign, although she has on occasion been made aware of it in the loft where she lives. She says that she sees some kind of a faint image, sort of a blur of white linen that swishes by her. In all, Vita has painted fifteen canvases of the entity and is planning a major exhibition of these and more at the Lerner Heller Gallery in New York.

Vita adds that she feels the spirit is a kindly one. It does not frighten her in any way, and she actually receives a family feeling about it. "My paintings are merely a kind of homage to her. After all, if Juliana was killed, the least I can do is paint her."

The vibrations of Juliana Sands continue in a place where she died. This is not at all uncommon in the case of a murder or an accident. The traumatic experience places the soul in such shock that it cannot accept "the other side" and remains. Again, remember that Vita was attracted to her loft, and while living in it, the vibrations of Juliana did appear to her. And the consequence was a series of magnificent paintings that will prove to be the making of Vita Girogi as an artist. Vita accepted the vibrations or energy field that had been a part of Juliana Sands and utilized them creatively, without being fearful of the emanations. Possibly, Juliana Sands was herself creative. Regardless, the vibrations remain, and more than one person has been made aware of this soul through the vibrations she left behind.

Going a step deeper, I believe that locations or houses can offer opportunities to fulfill certain karmic situations. In my own case, living in a certain house afforded me insight and enlightenment to more than one problem that I have brought into this life.

In 1969 I purchased a small home in the Catskill Mountain region of New York State. My first book had been a success, and more than anything I wanted to have a place away from the vibrations of New York City, someplace where I could get off to be alone, to meditate and write. I also had a strong inner voice telling me that it was time to experience owning my own home, although I have lived quite comfortably in apartments most of my life.

I had no idea where to look for a house, or for that matter, how to go about doing the same. I had visited the Bucks County area of Pennsylvania on several occasions and felt that this might be a good place to settle. The township of New Hope has many artists, writers, and other creative people in residence, and I began searching for a place there.

For several weeks I traveled the beautiful rustic country roads of Bucks County, never deciding on any of the houses I came across. Although many of them were quite lovely, none gave me that feeling that "this is my place, this is me."

In retrospect, I now realize that I had created a most improbable set of guidelines for a prospective home. It would be almost impossible to find all the things I demanded on my list, at least in one house, on one piece of property:

1. My home must not be too old, but not be of modern design.

2. There must be a great deal of acreage connected with the property on which the house would stand. I wanted privacy for writing and meditation.

3. The property should not be located in a town but close enough to one for a short drive.

4. Since swimming is one of the few sports I love, there would have to be water on the property—either natural or a pool.

5. The house must have a fireplace.

6. There must be a view from the house, either of a body of water or of mountains.

7. There must be a natural setting, with woods, streams, and wildlife.

8. The house and land must be quite inexpensive.

Naturally, with these demands in mind, I did not find a house. After many unsuccessful weekends in Bucks County, I gave up my search, at least for the time being. My friends pointed out to me that I most probably did not really want a home; this being the reason I set such high standards. I didn't agree. I somehow felt that if I was to invest in a home, it should have the things that would make me happy—and I wouldn't settle for less! "You're a true Taurus!" one of my friends exclaimed.

Several weeks later, at a party in New York City, I was introduced to a most excited couple who had just purchased a house in upstate New York, near

Kingston, the state's first capital. During conversation with the couple, I let them know of my experiences in a search for a home. They gave me the name of a real estate man they had been dealing with. "He's very nice," one of my new acquaintances said. "And its worth the trip up there just to see the magnificent scenery of the Catskills."

I put the real estate man's name and address on file when I got home. About a month passed and I soon found myself tuning in to the meeting I had had with the couple at that New York party. I went to my files, took out the name of the real estate man in Kingston, and phoned him. "I'd like to come up and take a look at any houses you might have in the area," I told him.

"Yes," he said in an unmistakable Swedish accent. "I will be glad to show you, I have several just now. Do you know how to travel to here by car?"

I informed the man that I didn't have a car.

"No car?" He exclaimed. "This is the country. If you do live here, you would have to have a car."

"Yes, I realize that," I said. "I have a license, but have never owned a car in New York."

"Then I will meet you at the bus stop, if this is okay with you," the real estate man replied.

"Fine, I will be at the bus depot around two and will call you upon my arrival."

The bus trip up was quite beautiful. It has since passed my mind dozens of times that millions of people live in dirty, crowded, polluted New York City without realizing that within an hour's drive is some

of the most magnificent scenery anywhere in the entire world. The Hudson River Valley and the Catskill Mountains outshine anything I have ever seen in all my travels as far as natural, breathtaking settings. The air is pure, the hills and valleys are green, and there are no crowds.

Upon my arrival at the bus stop, the real estate man and I shook hands. He immediately asked me what kind of a house I was looking for. I handed him my list of demands. He pulled over to the curb, parked, and took out his glasses.

"My God!" he almost shouted. "You don't want *much*, do you?"

I smiled a very weak smile, somewhat embarrassed.

The real estate man took off his cap and wiped his completely bald head with a handkerchief. "Okay, first stop is down the road a bit."

We traveled a few miles. The terrain looked familiar to me; that déjà vu feeling. This first house was in a shaded glen. It was a squared-off, plastic-looking modern structure.

"I don't think I even want to see the inside of this place," I said.

"I thought you wouldn't. But I wanted you to see what mostly is being built here at this time. This kind of thing is usually available around here and the price is quite high—can be over sixty thousand."

He gave me a sly smile and a wink, and we sped off. "Now I'll show you something that's just for you,

you can compare. That's why I took you to see that first place."

I bristled with quick anger. I despise this sort of sales technique. Then I thought, well, at least he was honest and told me what he was doing.

We drove about seven more miles, on a road that skirted a huge body of water. The road twisted and turned, uphill and down, around hairpin bends.

"This here on the right is the Ashokan Reservoir," my host exclaimed, reading the question I was about to ask. "It is the main source for New York City's drinking water, built in 1915. Can you imagine, it is piped from here down to there, over a hundred miles. There are several townships underneath that water. The city purchased this big valley, dammed it up, and let the natural waters from the mountains beyond fill it."

The road was now up and the view became more beautiful as we drove. Glimpses of the reservoir could be seen through the open spaces between the forest trees that covered its banks. We suddenly turned into a driveway and up a long, steep hill. At the end of the road was a charming house, set on a plateau, overlooking the water. Beyond the water was the beginning of the Catskill Mountain range.

"The sun sets behind those mountains," the real estate man said. "I've been here. We can check two things off your little list, right?"

I nodded affirmatively.

As we walked to the house, he told me that there

were seventeen acres connected with the house. "And they are all quite natural, as you can see."

The house was only eighteen years old. A fireplace had been installed within the past five years. There were six rooms, kitchen, and two baths. A hundred feet from the main house was a smaller, cabanalike building which had been erected beside a large swimming pool, set in the ground only a few years before.

It was my dream house! Everything is here, I thought. Then I realized that the price of such a place would be out of my range. This would be the block.

"How much?" I asked, closing my eyes tight.

The bald real estate man quoted the very low price. I stared at him. "Don't joke around," I said. "I really love this place. It has such possibilities."

"I'm not joking," he replied. "That's the price. They were asking much more a few months ago, but came down. The man is retired and wants to do some traveling, doesn't want to be tied down. So they dropped the price."

We met the owners and I made an instant decision. The papers were signed and I took out a mortgage in a local bank. In the literal sense of the word, the house was a steal. In fact, I felt somewhat guilty about giving such a low price.

I did not like the previous owners of the house. They were insensitive, quite backward, and left vibrations behind them that I am still trying to get rid of. But beyond their vibrations were all the positive qualifications of a home. I knew that I had been led to that house. It was mine.

On another level, unaware to me at the time, I was attracted to the house for karmic reasons—the house was going to be instrumental in so much awareness for me that in retrospect I am sure that I would not have purchased it had I known beforehand what was ahead of me.

I had lived in many places before, but never has any of them offered me experiences that would change my way of thinking, my way of life. Lessons began coming at me from the day I moved in.

In a short period of time, my "golden retreat" became a burden so overpowering it almost did me in. During my first few years there, several lawsuits were presented to me by unscrupulous merchants, automobile dealers, and laborers who either never completed their jobs or ripped me off in other ways.

Although all the evidence was in my favor, corrupt judges would settle cases against me. One judge called my adversary by his first name during the trial, stopped the proceedings, and had a talk with him about business! I was told by the lawyer who represented me that I was, after all, the outsider from New York City.

My friends were convinced that I must somehow be unconsciously choosing workers and merchants whom I knew would bring about negative results. Roxanne Dent, one friend who is very much involved in metaphysics, asked if I didn't go out of my way to hire the "bad guys." One case is still in the courts after four years, and still the job has not been done. Everywhere I turned, I was being placed in situations that would become negative. It got to the point where I wondered if the house was not cursed.

By nature, I am not a disciplined person. My career in the theater as a performer and writer came easy to me, as I had a natural talent, mostly a sharp wit. There wasn't too much need for discipline. I just did and performed what I wanted. As a professional psychic, my talents became known almost immediately to vast numbers of people through media exposure. Although I worked hard in both the theater and as a psychic, I never had to train or struggle for expression. When I needed something, it was there.

Consequently, although I was a success in both these areas, I feel I might have accomplished much more had I been able to discipline myself. I have always known that one of the main reasons for my being placed on the earth in this life was to acquire discipline—there is evidence that in past lives I squandered away many talents through an undisciplined attitude. By my living in the house I purchased, avenues would be made available to me that were not before. If I were at all suicidal, I would have done it during this period, and with some justification. The pressures at this time were overwhelming.

For a time, I started to hate the house, to resent

having bought it. I began to distrust my own psychic awareness in regards to my own best interests. Why the hell was I here? Why couldn't I have foreseen these terrible things? But as in most cases where tough situations have arisen in my life, I was not to have been aware *before* the situations were to take place. If I was aware, I would most probably have run the other way. But I learned to sustain myself through these experiences.

I disciplined myself to carry on. Only by disciplining my mind, body, and soul was I able to continue. I was literally *forced* to become more disciplined. And once a person works with discipline, it is impossible to go back in the other direction. No: the problems of the house were affording me the opportunity to seek out the uncompleted karma from past lifetimes.

As I looked deeper and searched longer, the discipline of keeping the house and facing the overpowering injustices gave me insight into myself. I was forced to grow up.

This was not the only lesson I had to learn through owning this particular house. A confrontation that was indeed karmic came to light.

I admit to having been a male chauvinist for the greater part of my life. It was a matter of my upbringing.

I was brought up to believe that women were indeed second-class citizens meant to be mothers, wives, housekeepers, and cooks, and to otherwise "look after" the men in a household: a woman is a woman and a man is a man and never the twain shall meet.

For most of my life, I had a complete lack of understanding for—nor did I care about—the role of women in our society.

I would argue against women's liberation advocates, feeling that those who were a part of women's liberation really desired to be men. To my way of thinking, women's lib consisted of those misfits of the female race who were frustrated, discontent, or just wished to wear the pants in the family, employment situations, and in general.

Like most men (or women) who did not understand the true ideals and goals of the women's liberation movement, I was in need of enlightenment. Unfortunately, opportunities for this needed understanding were not forthcoming. What was the worse for the matter was the fact that I did not even realize that I had a problem. I didn't outwardly believe that women were inferior to men; it was a part of my breeding, my childhood, and then my adulthood.

It was my house that was to be the key to my enlightenment in regards to women. Being on a mountain far away from the nearest city, it was not easy for me to get any help. I was forced to become a "housewife." Being single, I had no woman to do the necessary work that I thought women were born to do. Living in a house rather than an apartment is as different as is night to day.

Besides dusting, vacuuming, doing the laundry, ironing, feeding my numerous animals, I also had to do the "man's work"—caring for the lawn, getting firewood, plowing the snow from the driveway. It got to the point where I would stand by the kitchen sink and, looking out at the most beautiful view, would almost cry at the thought of having to do those "damn lousy dishes" once again. The same dishes, the same pots and pans—always dirty, always having to be cleaned. The same sink, and after a while, even the same view . . . endless. What about women who have several children? I began to think. What about my own mother, who brought up three children and ran a very large house that was always spotless, neat, and ready for anyone to be able to come in and be comfortable?

I did not feel free. I was a slave to the house. In truth, I was a housewife; I felt married to the house. And I hated it.

It was then that I realized what a woman's position is in our society. The drudgery of dusting the *same* furniture, vacuuming the *same* rug, cooking on the *same* stove . . . day after day, after day, after day. . . .

It amazed me that more women do not go berserk and murder their entire families.

So that is what it's all about? I'd say. This is what women are fighting for, to break the bondage of being *merely* a housewife trapped forever by the home. At least I had a chance to escape with my writing and when I gave lectures or made media appearances.

At one time, I was tired of being alone. I also needed someone to foot some of the bills, so I took in a boarder. If this didn't cinch the fact that I was in need of a karmic healing regarding the position of women, then nothing was.

At first my boarder was fine. But as time passed he began to act as if I were a typical housewife. Since he went to work on a daily basis and I was generally at home writing books and preparing my lectures, I was soon delegated the jobs of getting the house together, not only for myself but for him as well—clothes left all over the house, beds left unmade, cooking and cleaning up afterward, getting rid of the garbage.

One day my boarder came home and actually said, "We're having steak again? We just had steak yesterday." I threw it on the floor.

Sometimes he'd come home and ask what I did all day. I really do believe that he thought his clothes were washed, hung to dry, and ironed by some sleight-of-hand magic trick.

"I don't know why I have to do this work," he'd complain if I got him to do some housework. "You're home all day, and besides, you make most of the mess yourself."

Another time I complained that I didn't even have time for my writing anymore. "Can't you do that in your spare time? I mean, you're here all day. What can be taking so much time that you cannot delegate certain times to writing, other times to housework? You probably could even write as you do some of the light housework."

Expletive deleted!

As this sort of horror continued, I came to realize what the cry of the women's liberation movement truly means. Women are the garbage persons, the clean-up people, the maids in a family. I was placed in the position of being a "woman" and I hated it. But I would not have had the opportunity to see this had I not been attracted to this particular house. The house in its specific location attracted me to it. It was not until years later that I came to realize the true attraction, the karmic need I had to live there.

4

The Curse of Geography

There is too much evidence that vibrations can be effective and do remain in certain areas, created by people who—consciously or unconsciously—have made them a reality.

D: Certain geographic areas, I believe, do have specific vibrations, and certain individuals can pick up on these vibrations, whether good or bad. I know of a family that were about to move into a new home and they all loved the house excepting for one of the children, the youngest in fact. This one child sensed something negative in the vibrations of the house, but could not express what it was other than what he felt. On some level of awareness the child was tuned in to the vibrations of the house. As it was, the family later found out that the previous owners of the house were indeed negative people, that there had been much negative energy expressed there, and that finally some violence had taken place between the husband and the wife that culminated in their breaking up and selling the house. I know that certain places make me very upset, although nothing has ever happened to me in them, or to anyone I know. I just feel the vibrations of negation in them.

I have a friend Matt, an editor of a large publishing concern. Matt had been invited to spend a summer weekend in a very rural section of Minnesota with an author friend who is quite well known. The author I'll call Gene. Gene is quite robust, extremely enthusiastic, and has many interests. He has a great capacity for understanding and believes in ESP, although he is cautious in such matters.

On this particular weekend, Gene was holding open house and had invited two well-known psychics who also happened to be friends. Gene was considering the purchase of an old farm just outside of town and hoped that the people he had invited might be able to "psyche out" the place. After dinner, all his guests took a ride out to see the farm.

It was twilight and the crickets were chirping while the evening's first bats were ricocheting through the air. Everyone was charmed by the natural beauty of the place: tall grass and thistles, rolling green hills studded with ancient oak and hickory trees. A beautiful limestone cliff with a spring lay beyond the next ridge, and closer to the road was the original farmhouse, overgrown with trees and weeds. There was also a huge barn on the property, its boards weathered gray but still structurally sound for renovation. The two well-known psychics looked around and declared that the place was tranquil and quiet. "It's full of peaceful vibrations," one of them exclaimed.

But Matt realized from previous experience that the normally optimistic and serene psychics tend to look on the bright side of situations, so he got off by himself for a few moments of meditation. He asked himself, "Is there anything Gene ought know about this place?"

Matt then had an odd reaction, for he automatically swiveled his head and "locked in" his gaze on a small stand of gnarled and rather dry-looking oaks down a slope about a hundred yards from where he stood. Without informing the others, Matt went down to the area he had zeroed in on. He felt a sudden shortness of breath. At first he attributed this to the cigarette he was smoking. But then he realized that the walk was *downhill* and therefore a simple puff of tobacco could not account for his inability to catch his breath.

There was nothing unusual that Matt could make of the area physically. The scruffy little grove of trees was neither imposing nor majestic. But the closer he got to the spot, the tighter his chest became. He described it as a "suffocating sense of visceral awe, as if I were entering the territory of someone—or something—of incredible power."

When he got to the edge of the grove, he stopped. The sensation of a presence was not particularly localized; whatever was responsible for the feeling extended in a diameter of fifty feet or so, with the grove as its rough center. It became really difficult for Matt to draw a full breath. Trying to account for it psychically, he got the distinct impression of a man's body lying flat in the grass, with the breath crushed out of him. But he received nothing more, and went back to rejoin the rest of the group.

Very casually, he asked the psychics if they got any impressions from the specific area he had just been in. They said that they didn't, that the place was still to be "read" as serene and benevolent.

Later, Matt told his impression to Gene and apologized for being the "party pooper" in the bunch, erroneously picking up bad vibes.

Gene patted him on the back and said that there wasn't any harm done. Most probably he had been picking up on some Indian who had died there in centuries past. Matt shrugged it off with the rationalization that no one is perfect; the next day he drove home.

About a week passed when Gene phoned Matt with some quite unexpected news. On the night that they had all gathered to "psyche out" the place, one of his friends had left early because his wife "couldn't stand the feeling of the place." Another woman had said that she had a fleeting glimpse of a man hanging from the gable of the barn with a noose around his neck. Then, a few days later, Gene had driven two other quite aware friends to the property. Each of them had received negative vibrations such as those that Matt had tried to articulate.

Gene had then checked with the local police chief about the property, hoping to get its history. The officer confirmed the fact that a man had hanged himself in the barn one night following a dance. In talking with other residents of the area, Gene also discovered that there had been a shotgun murder and suicide in the farmhouse. It didn't seem to matter, however, since Gene's bid for the property had been turned down by the present owners.

Matt listened to the stories over the phone and began to receive more psychic impressions about the property. His feeling was that the killings were not the *cause* of the trouble, but a by-product. Matt felt that there was a vibration of some kind in that grove of trees that he had received the negative response from.

"Whatever it is," Matt said, "does not want anyone on the property. It considers the entire farm its own property. And it *is* incredibly powerful." Matt said that if Gene indeed wanted that farm, he would have to make peace with whatever it was in the grove.

A week later, Gene called Matt with the news that he had listened to the advice given to him about the farmhouse. "I went out there with my two sons," Gene told Matt. "It was a hot August day, but as soon as I walked into that grove, it became ice cold. Rick was off playing somewhere, but I had my other son, Tim, with me. We sat down, and as you told me to do, I simply spoke into the air, telling or assuring 'It' that we recognized its claim to ownership of the property; that we didn't plan to chop down any trees or make any other physical changes on the place; that we respected its ownership and wanted only to share the land for our own lifetime, realizing that it was the permanent owner. . . .

"At that instant, the cold left and it became warm again. Tim, who is quite tuned in himself, leaped into the air and swore that he felt something hug him.

"I went away for a week, on business, and when I got back, the lawyer was on the phone saying that the family had reconsidered my bid, and that I could have the property if I still wanted it." Gene did purchase the farm.

A year passed and Matt asked about the property and its vibrations. Gene replied that whatever it was in the grove seemed to tolerate him and his family, but any visitors or friends that came to the house were made decidedly uncomfortable.

As it turned out, a renovation of the house and the barn would have been far too costly. Gene sold the property to a farmer who wished to use it for pasture. He was not sorry for getting rid of the land. The vibrations were far too negative.

Apparently, there were vibrations of someone (likely more than one person) who had lived there before and were still making claim to it via some psychic manifestations most upsetting to those who either lived or visited there. My own psychic feeling is that if they were to dig deeply on the land, especially in the vicinity of the grove, it would be discovered that the area was an ancient sacred Indian burial ground, protected from any intervention by those Indians who placed their dead in the ground after much ritualistic protection was afforded the deceased. Like the pyramids in Egypt, this area in Minnesota had been given protection by people who knew how to crcatc a vibratory field of energy over a place. The resting places of the dead were not meant to be tampered with.

The vibrations of the Egyptian pyramids have always fascinated me. The "curse of the Pharaohs" inscribed on the tomb seals and the walls had been created by those who practiced the art of controlling vibratory energy. It cannot be mere coincidence that more than twenty persons connected at some time or another with the uncovering of Tutankhamen's tomb have died under most unusual, sometimes mysterious, circumstances.

Howard Carter, the archaeologist responsible for the excavation of the famous tomb in Egypt's Valley of the Kings, died before most of the finds could be brought to the surface. But it was the deaths of three other Egyptologists who visited the tomb for one reason or another that gave rise to the legend of the "curse."

Immediately after the opening of the inner chamber of the tomb on February 17, 1923, Lord Herbert Carnarvon, a well-known collector, world traveler, and partner of Carter, developed lassitude, headaches, breathlessness, and enlarged glands. His health deteriorated rapidly until he died on April 6. It was said that Carnarvon was a victim of a mosquito bite, but Carnarvon had lived in Egypt for many years and traveled the world many times over. It is therefore unlikely that he should have died from an insect bite, having had thousands of such bites in his lifetime.

Arthur Mace, assistant director of the New York Department of Egyptian Antiquities, and George Benedite of the Louvre in Paris, both visited the tomb and then died suddenly. Lord Westbury, secretary to Carter when the tomb was being discovered, jumped to his death from his seventh-floor apartment in London. His son was found dead in his bed, having retired in perfect health the night before. There has never been an explanation of his death. Archibald Douglas Ried, another Egyptologist, died as he was about to X-ray one of the Egyptian mummies. Arthur Weigall, who also assisted in excavating the tombs of Egypt, suddenly became ill and died. It is this quick succession of out-of-the-ordinary deaths to those who dug up the tombs that proves that there indeed was some force of energy, some vibratory field, that had been created to protect the buried kings.

Not only houses, apartments, or buildings, but specific geographic areas have vibrations that could be negative or positive for the person. A location can be holding one back from advancement, be it spiritual, mental, or physical.

In ancient China, people would consult an oracle before they built a house. The mystic would go to the prospective geographic area and feel out the vibrations, trying to see if the location was a good one for the person who sought this advice. Often before buying land the oracle would be brought to a proposed house building site and asked if the vibrations were conducive to a good life for the prospective owner. Today Pennsylvania Dutch *Hexenmeisters* still align their houses and beds with true north on the compass. This assures them of a true energy flow that is most positive.

In my own work, I have been asked to get impressions on prospective individual homesites. I once worked for a construction company, choosing areas that would be most successful as opposed to sites that had negative vibrations emanating from them.

For that matter, there are entire geographic locations that are positive and many that are negative. As V. said, "Cities give off vibrations to me. Although I live near Boston, I can't stand to go there. I sense confusion; I get a mixed-up feeling. Whenever I have to drive through Boston, I always get a headache. We live in a world of vibrations, constantly picking up on them, consciously or unconsciously, and if we only considered them for what they are and accept them, we would avoid a great deal of negation in our lives."

A person might be a complete failure in one section of a country and a tremendous success in another location. The vibrations of one place may be conducive to that person's energy and trigger health, opportunity, or some form of advancement. In like manner, another location can have the opposite, negative effect.

When I first began giving psychic consultations, I found that I would sometimes tell certain people that they should move from their present location. "Are you planning a move?" I might ask.

"Not that I know of" was a frequent reply.

"Well, you should be moving. I sense that a move would bring about the positive results you are seeking. You will never be a success where you presently are."

I discovered that this impression of having someone move to another location came up quite often. When I would get feedback from those I did feel should move from their present locations, the results were mostly good.

An example of this was Howard Butley, a young man who came to me for a consultation back in 1969. Howard was an aspiring artist. Every avenue he took in regards to his artwork came to naught. He would have long "dry" periods in which he would be completely unable to create.

In his mind he was always wishing to leave, to get away from it all, to be far away from where he was: "I'm really not content. Maybe it's the artist's luck to be discontented with himself, his world. But I don't like it, and I don't know what to do about it. My work suffers. I go for months unable to lift a hand to the canvas," Howard Butley related to me during the reading.

"Did you ever think of going to another country?" I asked.

"Sure, but it's the same there," Howard said. "I went to Europe once and it was even more negative. You can't run away from yourself, I found."

"Do you believe in reincarnation?" I inquired of the confused man who sat facing me in my office.

"Well, I've done some reading, and a lot of it does make sense. I don't disbelieve, nor do I believe in it completely."

"Psychically, I feel that you have brought your artistic ability from another lifetime. And you are working to express it in this life. I perceive that in your most previous life you were not Caucasian. You were of the Indian race. Not American Indian, East Indian."

The young man looked at me with an expression of deep understanding. "Wow!" he exclaimed. "I'm very much taken with the Indian way of life. I've done some yoga and tried transcendental meditation. I really like the Indian culture and especially the artwork. In fact, the one sculpture I sold was Indian in form. But what does this mean to me now, in this life?"

"You are unconsciously recalling the place where you were in the last life. Your subconscious yearns for some karma to be completed, something that was not completed there before. You did not fulfill your karmic reason for being in that life. It was cut short by some natural disaster. Unconsciously, you are struggling to get back to India, to the place where you had been working out your karma."

I had been in a semitrance state while giving this young man the desired information. I could hear Indian music—chimes, brass bells, finger rings, and drums.

"So, that's what you feel," Howard Butley said. "I find that most interesting. I will have to check it out."

We talked some more and the consultation came to an end. It wasn't until two years later that I received a letter addressed to me through my publisher. The letter reads:

> *Dear Dan, didn't know where else to reach you, so I thought I might try your publisher. As you can see, I*

am in India. I thought a lot about what you said on the day I saw you almost two years ago. Things got worse for me after I saw you. My natural attraction for India plus your enlightenment put me on a course for that country. I guess that you confirmed something that was in my mind. The good news is that since I have been here I have changed my outlook—greatly. It was something like coming home here. I felt very comfortable, relaxed and was able to start painting again. I have had one exibition already in which about 75 percent of my paintings were sold! I have taken to painting old Indian buildings with the moon behind them at night. Almost all those who have bought the paintings have been Indians. Many who came into the gallery asked to meet the artist and were quite surprised when they were introduced to me. They thought that they were going to meet an Indian, as the work does have that quality, form, and execution. I guess, according to you, they were right. I have been delving into the teachings of reincarnation and find myself not at all surprised at what I discover. It is like I have learned it before and this is a refresher course. Regardless, I am now the person I had wanted to be but couldn't in any other places where I have lived. My vibrations are much like that of India, and the people accept me here. I have found my rightful place and just wanted to let you know that I have. With love, Howard Butley.

Howard Butley did have a strong karmic tie with a certain location and was not able to complete his destiny without being in that place. It is not always the case of a need to complete karma in a certain location, but it does happen. If at all possible, reincarnation should be considered in regards to where one makes his home. Many people who are unsuccessful in life do not realize that it is simply a matter of being in a location that is not compatible with their personal vibratory level. A geographic change will, in many instances, remove the person from the incompatibile vibrations.

In New York, a friend of mine was rather a Milquetoast sort of person—physically frail, somewhat effeminate, and very nonaggressive. Recently, when he changed the vibrations of his locale by a move to Los Angeles, he became a completely different person—stronger in his approach to life, more aggressive regarding what he wants for himself, much more outgoing and sociable. Even his physical appearance took on changes; his body became more masculine and his face filled out and changed shape. It was an astounding emergence, and I feel that it is all due to the vibrations of one place as opposed to another. On a recent visit to his former home, he fell into some old ways and habits and couldn't wait to get back to his new home and life in California. You may have noticed that there are places that attract you very strongly, or others that have a repelling effect.

Personally, I did not like southern California

when I lived there for a period of time. Even though I really liked the place physically, the vibrations were all wrong for me. Negation seemed to grow right up alongside those palms that are in actuality *not* indigenous to California. On the other hand, the northern part of California, especially San Francisco, held most perfectly simpatico vibrations for me. I had a feeling of being a part of the area.

But I feel Japan is home to me; I am comfortable there. I vibrate and glow. My inner peace is always at hand; it does not have to be worked on. Meditation comes easy. In America I have to work at everything and everything seems a struggle for me: I am at odds here in the country where I was born. The vibrations of Japan and my own are much alike, and it is true that like attracts like. I have met many spiritual-minded people who hated Japan, detesting the people, and never felt one moment of "belonging." The vibes were not right for them.

I am sure that this psychic attraction to or dislike of an area happens with most people. If you can only become aware of it, much heartbreak could be avoided by going along with your feelings about a specific location, either positive or negative.

5

The Soul
of Art
and Music

"Your generation coined the expression 'vibes,' " I told the younger people in my development group, "the generation before you used other terms. I notice the music young people are into; when they talk about this music they refer to vibes. Say that there are three rock groups and that they play very similar music. It seems that the young people will choose one of those three and say, 'Wow! Far out! That band has really great vibes.' At the same time one of the other bands might be tabbed as having bad vibes. To many people, the music of both groups might sound almost exactly the same, and yet only one band is chosen. I've been witness to complete adulation being heaped on one group and outright disdain being expressed for another, at the same concert, even though to me the music seemed quite similar. Is it in truth the vibrations of a group or an individual singer that is the attraction, rather than the music itself? Can you explore that a bit? What is it that you feel at a rock concert that makes you like one group and despise another? What is it that turns you off? Is it the music? Is there that much difference in rock bands?

A.: It's what a particular group is *expressing* with their music.

E.: When you think about the recent pop artists, such as the Mamas and the Papas, Cat Stevens, Carley Simon, they made you feel good. They expressed themselves, their vibes were good, and you picked up on it.

A.: Performers like Cat Stevens, Donovan, Joni Mitchell, don't *just* make you feel good, they are very emotional singers.

Logan: Well, Alice Cooper is emotional. . . .

A.: But it's a completely different emotion. You take the Alice Coopers, the David Bowies, and others like that and they reflect negative vibes through their music. It's from the lower level of feeling that expresses our anger, hatred, sadism, and all that negative stuff. These vibrations come across to us in their music. Whereas the others send out positive emotional vibrations, I believe.

Logan: That's doubly interesting because music does emanate physical vibrations.

A.: Right, and when a performer expresses himself with his own soul experience and puts it into his music, it is double . . . I, mean, like vibrations on vibrations.

K.: I feel that the acid-rock performers express gross materialism in their work—everything relates to the material in their music. It isn't *only* sex. And they are selfish, they perform to please themselves. Everything is pleasure-seeking and self-gratification. This is the kind of vibrations that are sent out by a great many acid-rock performers. There's no self-control, no discipline.

Logan: If these bands emanate such bad vibes, why are they so popular?

A.: Well, I guess that there are people who like it. Maybe it's *like* attracting *like*, I mean, the vibes of Alice

Cooper attract audiences that have the same kind of vibrations that he has—negative!

K.: Their message is total selfishness, and that's the kind of people they attract to themselves—their fans.

R.: A lot of people feel that the lower, undeveloped emotional aspects should be enhanced. These negative emotions are, after all, the stronger ones. And some acquaintances of mine feel that they get more of a charge, more sensation, if they indulge themselves in the stronger emotions. I think that the Alice Cooper type groups indulge in the negative emotional type of music; the physical is all-important to them. If you sit around and pinch yourself, you can actually *feel* that pinching. It's easier than trying to get in touch with yourself. People who are really frightened of getting in touch with themselves have a performer on stage saying, "Hey, it's really good! It doesn't matter, this is what you really want"—death, murder, wild sex, and the like. They respond to that.

Logan: Maybe that's why I have heard such violent discussions regarding rock groups and individual performers. There seems to be no middle road. Either the performers have good vibes and they are followed, or they have bad vibes and you stay away. But as you said, like attracts like, so the negatively vibed performers do have their followings who see them as having good vibes—at least for them.

A.: I guess that would sum it up. I think that those people who are attracted to the negative rock music can relate to the music because that is where they are at personally, where their heads are at. Like vibrations attract like vibrations.

D. (age thirty-five): And when you attend one of these far-out rock concerts, just look around and see how many people are responding to the vibrations of negation. They become hypnotized by the ugly vibrations being created by the rock group and they begin to act in a like manner. The air at a rock concert is usually filled with an anxiety, anticipation. If you are working in any kind of positive frame of mind or awareness the vibrations at one of these rock concerts can make you literally ill. Drugs are used to enhance the negative trip and act as a battery charger of sorts for these negative vibrations. Many kids take the negative vibrations that are created at rock concerts out with them onto the streets. There is usually much damage to personal property in the vicinity of an acid-rock concert; the negative vibrations prevail. Some of the kids take the negation home with them and do numbers on their families. . . . It's really a very bad scene.

Logan: If this is true, then the young audiences of today have taken a big step forward in awareness, most probably unconsciously. They are in truth recognizing the performers' soul expression and that's, to quote a phrase, very heavy! When the generation before you, myself included, chose a performer or a group, they were chosen on looks or a particular sound in their music—in other words, the material, obvious aspects that are always apparent. But your generation seems to want to get to the soul of a performer. To feel what kind of individual vibrations the performers are emitting seems more important than the performing and music itself.

A.: I have discovered that most of the people I can relate to like the exact same kind of music that I like—even if I just meet them, there seems to be some common ground there. Whereas we also seem to agree on what turns us off.

It's like what you were saying earlier. If I walk into a stranger's house and flip through his records, I can tell where that person is at. I mean, if that person has a lot of acid rock—the Rolling Stones, loud, glitter-rock music—I can make an instant judgment that I won't get along with that person. I am usually always correct on this, because that is where they are at in their heads. It is their expression as well as the performers on the records.

R.: I think that you really can't make a judgment by looking at a person's record collection or his books. You just can't look at these things and yell, "Ahh, that's where they are at!" These people might be able to relate to the music they like on a completely different level than you do.

A.: Sure, but I'm looking at it from my point of view.

Logan: It's almost like psychoanalyzing someone, this making a kind of judgment on them based on their music.

A.: Psychoanalyzing without all the crap.

K.: Yes, I believe that. And I do agree that the vibrations of specific kinds of music can tell you where a person's head is at. Personally, for instance, the vibrations of acid rock annoy the hell out of me. First of all I have a physical reaction to the acid-rock sound. I get itchy and really can't stay in a room where acid rock is being played for any length of time. The negative vibrations of the music played usually do extend to the people listening to it. I am usually turned off by those who dig rock music to any degree.

Logan: Well, then, are you usually correct in your initial feeling of the vibrations that you might get from a person's record collection? I mean, if you do find that a person has all acid-rock records and then for one reason or another you have had to be with this person over an extended period of time, does your initial judgment prove correct?

A.: Yes, I have had acquaintances like that and it has proven to be so. I didn't like their music and I discovered over a period of time that we had very little in common, that the person thinks quite differently than I do. I have had to really search other means of communication. It has proven most difficult.

R.: A lot of acid rock is created to enhance a drug trip. There are things in acid rock that if you are not stoned on drugs you do not hear, or you just don't notice when you're not high. And so, if people constantly listen to this kind of music all the time, I would say they are into drugs.

E.: A friend's husband is into acid rock and drugs, and this attraction to the kind of negative music he likes is carried over into almost all other areas of his life. His love for this type of music is definitely carried over into how he acts, thinks, and expresses himself.

A.: Well, I have found that people into acid-rock music do have a lot in common. My acquaintances and friends are all divided into separate groups; people that I like, am comfortable with, are not into drugs or wild sex. They all definitely do not like the kind of music that we are now talking about—in fact, they hate it.

Logan: Then you would say that there is some kind of connection in the music and their lives.

A.: Definitely. So it isn't that you're making a judgment on the music they like and have in their houses. It's more than that. The music is a reflection of how they react in other things that they do. The philosophy in the music is what gets to them and they follow it. The music has vibrations and they in turn use this music to build up their own vibrations, and they are negative.

Logan: Let's change the subject for a moment. N. is an artist. In relation to art, vibrations might mean something else. What exactly?

N.: Take, for example, one particular painting and the vibrations that one can pick up from it. It's the whole painting itself: the physical reality of that painting. It's the organization of the composition, the integration of the colors, the concept—all of this together has a gestalt, a wholeness. This painting is a complete entity in the true sense of the word, and being an entity, it gives off its own specific vibration.

Then there is the response to the painting by different people. You run the gamut of all kinds of different responses. A great painting very consistently evokes certain responses from most people, and usually strong ones, either positive or negative. The painting will say many different things to many different people who pick up from it certain vibrations and interpret them according to their own level of awareness.

Logan: Could this be an example of what you are talking about? I am attracted to, yet also horrified to the very depths of my being, by anything Van Gogh has ever painted. When I was a youngster I knew nothing about Van Gogh's life or work, but when I first saw one of his paintings back then—the one with the sun rising over a blowing field—I was thrown into a state of near hysteria. I had nightmares about that painting just from looking at it. And later, his other works never failed to upset me. I could never have a Van Gogh in my home; I believe that I would become too depressed. Is that what you mean? That I, in some way, picked up the vibrations of the artist's "being" from viewing his works?

N.: Precisely. The reason that Van Gogh's work has this effect on almost everyone was his rare talent. He could communicate to you so very thoroughly, exactly where his head was at. He imbued his work with his soul, or his vibrations, if you will. The underlying reality of a painting is what an artist is expressing, what he is feeling. This is a measure of his talent; that he can communicate a part of himself, his vibes, to you.

Logan: Then it's really nothing that can be learned.

N.: It's not learned. All of the arts come out of very basic, fundamentally shared awarenesses—as human beings.

Logan: Van Gogh was considered to have been insane and I do think that his insanity comes through in his work. How could he have transmitted this to a painting?

N.: When we try to define achievement, or talent, in regard to this one artist and his work, I believe it was his ability to express *exactly*, to communicate *exactly*, the condition of his mind, his soul, his vibrations. What we call a great artist, or a great performer, or a great musician, is actually the skill in the given medium that one uses so effectively.

Logan: Do you think that artists with perhaps superior technical skill than Van Gogh will never achieve that feeling of reaching out from the canvas with their inner selves, their vibrations, because they are afraid to have other people see their true selves laid bare? So they actually conjure up a different way of painting, almost as a cover-up for what they are truly feeling or experiencing?

N.: Of course: and that's extremely complex. Take Dali, for example. Looking at his work, you could never detect where Dali was at emotionally at the time he was creating a particular painting. His work is so conceptional, very intellectual. His obvious intent was *not* to communicate himself . . . he had a concept he wanted to communicate, rather than his own personal feelings.

Logan: In this case he worked to extricate himself from his creation. Is that what you are saying?

N.: That's right.

Logan (*laughing*): Maybe that's why I don't like his work.

N.: Most probably. That's what can turn some people away, this lack of the artist's vibrations in his work. But there again, for people who do not want to be in touch with themselves, who are looking for a perfectly executed concept, Salvador Dali is marvelous.

Logan: But on the other hand, this cover-up of feelings has become a part of the artist, so that in truth what one is seeing is the artist's expression, even if it is a conceptional, perfectly executed work.

N.: Yes, and that is a most complex area. You know, as I said in the beginning, there is the entity of the painting and then the responses the painting evokes. Although Dali paints in a conceptional and intellectual way devoid of personal emotion, it is still Dali expressing himself. I've always felt that one problem of establishing objective criteria for measuring the quality of a work of art has been in this enormous variety of personal reaction or response. It's a very fundamental reason why we shouldn't have censorship. The Russian official position on art is so outrageous because it narrows down and limits so very much. Artists have got to have a wide-open range where we can have a Van Gogh and a Dali or Cézanne. . . .

Logan: Well, I know little about art, but if I walked into a room with one painting by Dali and another by Van Gogh, I would immediately be attracted to the Van Gogh. It would be a gut reaction. On the other hand, if I desired to intellectualize and knew quite a bit about art and how it has developed throughout history, I would probably take more time with the Dali. I think most people would be like that. The vibrations would emanate from the Van Gogh first; you would be pulled into its orbit whether you liked the painting or not. Whereas with the Dali, one must have some background in art, a course in art appreciation.

N.: That applies to all modern painting.

Logan: That is what I objected to when I was an actor—this method style of acting. For example, I would see an actor who was tremendously exciting, whose vibrations literally leaped from him to the audience. In many instances I was completely overwhelmed by the vibrations being sent out by this performer. Then I would see people who have gone through the method style of acting and I would be aware of their technique. I knew what and how they were trying to portray emotionally, and this is what I object to in Dali. He has great technique, but the energy of the artist, the very thing that I feel makes a work of art, is missing. The painting or the performance is somehow devoid of the creator. The artist almost works to do away with the emotion, the personal vibrations. I studied the method type of acting for a time and decided it was wrong for me—this trying to become the character you portray, other than yourself. It's not acting, it's something else. In fact, if you do indeed become someone else, when you are acting you're insane.

E.: There are two famous concert violinists —Jascha Heifetz and Isaac Stern. Of the two, Heifetz is probably technically better, but Stern's playing sends me. I adore this man and his work. His playing comes from his soul, and the vibrations he sends out to an audience are something fantastic. He plays with such feeling! On the other hand, Heifetz always seemed cold to me; he plays a technically superb violin, but lacks the deep, emotional, vibratory feeling. The comparison between these two men has always been evident to me of the different vibrations that can emanate from one particular musician and not from the other.

Logan: Do you feel that you could tell the difference in a recording of the same piece as performed by Heifetz or Stern?

E.: Definitely, yes, I can, even from a recording.

N.: It's like with Van Gogh. You can *still* pick up the vibrations of the man even though he painted some pictures more than a hundred years ago.

Logan: Maybe we should reevaluate the rock groups of today. Possibly these musicians are attempting to get back to performing from the soul, the complete utilization of their emotional drive, the act of creating a vibratory force between themselves and their audiences. We have become so technically advanced in the arts, music especially, that maybe the rock groups try to get a primitive sound shouting, "Hey, this is me! This is *my* vibrations I'm sending out—raw and emotional, completely honest, no frills; this is where I am." Maybe this is what their desire is, rather than going to music school for ten years and playing a perfectly modulated and executed piece that they really don't care about, don't believe in—music that doesn't reflect themselves but someone else.

6

The Colors of Judy Garland

Color seems to be a characteristic of the vibrations of matter, and our souls seem to reflect it in this three-dimensional world through atomic patterns. We are patterns, and we project colors, which are there for those who can see them.

Edgar Cayce

I can often see color in the aura of individuals or geographic locations. On Harbour Island the auras of the natives were mostly blue-greens, violets, and shades of yellow—all positive, creative colors. In New York I couldn't help but take note of how many gray auras there were. Gray in an aura indicates to me a lack of spirituality, often lack of a life force itself. Gray is usually around those persons who have given up, resigned themselves to living in spiritual limbo. They are either afraid or unable to let go of the negative, materialistic aspects of their lives.

The first time that I can recall perceiving color in an aura was at a concert performed by Judy Garland in New York City. I was a devoted fan of Miss Garland. The vibratory level that she utilized in her performances overwhelmed an audience. In fact the energy that this woman exuded while onstage was frightening. I believe that many people who attended Judy Garland's shows were actually mesmerized in the truest meaning of the word. Unfortunately, Judy Garland did not know how to control this energy, how to guard it, or how to regenerate it. Eventually, this energy destroyed her.

It was a warm night in the middle of May 1959. Weeks before the concert, several friends and I waited on line for hours to get tickets. The performance was to take place at the old Metropolitan Opera House, and the only available seats were in the back of the mezzanine. We took them.

There are times in one's life when everything that happens can be recalled later at any given instant. For me, that night in May 1959 was one of them. I can recall in total every move that I made from the hour of 5 P.M. until I went home and to bed around 1:30 A.M. the next morning. It was like being on some fantastic drug. The vibrations that were built up in the audience and on the stage that night had entered my own consciousness and carried me through several hours that would be as memorable as any I would ever have.

Within blocks of the massive theater, one could sense an energy, a force that seemed to draw like a magnet. Hundreds of people were milling around the Metropolitan. Many had seats, just as many did not. Those who did not had been drawn there by the excitement, the magnetic pull that was a part of the Garland energy. We were nearly crushed by the throngs that jostled each other.

Once inside the building you could slice the vibrations of anticipation with a knife. It was as though these hundreds of people were gathering up energy from within themselves. Once it was amassed they could direct it at their idol, who at that point in her life was overweight and on the verge of a physical and mental breakdown. At least, this was the way that Judy Garland appeared. And due to the media coverage of her illnesses, her suicide attempts, her financial troubles, everyone knew it. She needed help, support, and her fans were there to give it to her. As the orchestra would strike up the overture of her standard hit songs, the audience reaction bordered on mass hysteria. On the night I waited to see Judy Garland from the mezzanine of the Metropolitan Opera house, I had become almost sick even before she came out. My head was light and I was dizzy. I was picking up on the furious energy created by the audience. By the time Garland appeared, the vibrations of hundreds, sometimes thousands, of people were right there with her. When Garland appeared at the end of her overture, it was as though Moses had opened the Red Sea; the sound of the applause, whistles, and shouts was actually deafening. Now the energy was being released.

As I watched Garland cross the stage to the microphone, I couldn't help note that she was in a red light—shades of dark red toward the outer edge and becoming more pink closer to her body.

"Why did they have to put that ugly red light on her?" I asked one of my friends.

"What red light?" my friend demanded. He turned to look at me as if I had taken leave of my senses.

Maybe this dizzy feeling I had was creating

images and lights, I reasoned with myself. But the more I looked, the more I could see of the light. Could that be her aura? I thought. I had been aware of auras before, but never with color. Usually, I could sense a bright glow around the person giving off the energy, but it was colorless.

As the performance continued, one could feel that Judy Garland was getting energy from her audience. At first she seemed stiff, somewhat off-key, not quite with the music. But as she got into the second number, it was as though she had become a different person—loose, staying on pitch, hitting every note right on.

It is my belief that Judy Garland fed off the energy that each audience would bring into the theater. It was the audiences who created the fantastic flow of energy she needed in order to build and sustain the electric magnetism that was so much a part of her every performance.

When she was onstage, Judy Garland was not only able to perform but able to become a force of energy that overcame every negative influence that was so much a part of her real life. Garland would often come from her dressing room shaking, a nervous wreck, sometimes vomiting. But the instant she got zapped by that energy field waiting for her onstage, she would become a completely alert, musically correct performer. Only onstage did she become a healthy, well-balanced human being.

If Judy Garland were to stumble in front of her

audience, or if she had to strain to reach a high note, the audience would generate more energy and send it to her so that she could get through the show. It was incredible—a kind of mystical ritual: the audience gave her energy, she took it and used it to build her own, and would then send it back to the crowd. In retrospect, Judy Garland was like a psychic vampire.

Judy Garland's daughter, Liza Minnelli, is a far better technician than her mother. She dances and sings as the trained performer that she is. But there is something missing: that energy, the vibrations that Judy Garland created and utilized. Garland had an electrified radiance and could make an entire audience cry like children or roar with laughter that sounded like the noise of a subway train.

The astute biographer Gerold Frank hit upon Garland's tremendous psychic energy in his memorable work *Judy* (Harper & Row, 1975):

> *But when she appeared onstage, heavy as she was, what did it all matter once she felt the audience reaction? Then she became, once more, an irresistible force. Fat as she was, and sick as she was—she would be in a hospital, near death, as the year ended—onstage she was giving more than a performance. She was giving a championship battle, a battle to win every person in every seat. She would burst backstage, perspiring, winded, fists clenched, early in the show. "Who put that goon in the first row? He's not even applauding! I'd like to belt him*

one!" Then, a dash of cold water over her face, a hurried rubbing with a towel, a gulp of whiskey with water, a quick warning—"I'll nail him! I swear I'll nail him!"—and back to the fray, to the arena, to shattering applause. Until, under the bombardment of her songs, her projection, the daggers of energy she directed at every single soul, the man she aimed at broke and, like the others, was standing, applauding, not knowing why.

I have seen people faint at Garland concerts. I saw staid, older businessmen types fall on their knees and weep at the foot of her stage. Once I went to a concert with two friends who did not particularly like Judy Garland. At the end of the show, they were both jumping up and down on their seats, screaming with delight. There is no doubt about it, Judy Garland unconsciously created a vibratory force between herself and her audiences that would engulf everyone within the radius of the place where she was performing. Even those people waiting outside the theater, unable to get tickets, seemed to be in some kind of energized trance. The energy level was so high that I do not think anything like it has ever been before or since.

A quarter of the way into her concert, I saw that the light around Garland was now light pink. Midway through, the color again changed into a very light green, then a darker green, which suddenly became an emerald green. By the time the concert was over,

Judy Garland was bathed in a deep blue. It was an extraordinary display, almost as fantastic as Garland's performance.

After a performance, Garland was exhausted. Her audience was even more exhausted. Creating such high pitched vibrations and sustaining them for long periods of time would take its toll on performer and fans alike.

It wasn't until many years later, after having investigated the teachings of the occult from ancient mystics through Edgar Cayce, that I became aware of the meaning of colors in regards to auras and vibrations. When I started to give readings myself, I trained to sense the colors around those who came to have consultations. It was actually more than ten years before the colors I had thought were so mysterious around Judy Garland had any meaning to me.

The initial color I saw surrounding Garland had been a dark red. This color represents inner turmoil. It is also a strong, vibrant color, indicating emotional instability and high temper. These characteristics were indeed very much a part of Garland at that time in her life. When I sensed the color changing to a lighter hue of red, this indicated an impulsive, self-centered person. Later the pink in her aura meant an immaturity, a childishness. When Garland worked onstage she did become quite childlike.

As the evening progressed her aura had much green in it. This meant that energy was being supplied. Green is the color of ego and of growth. It also governs the mental realm. As the color became a darker shade of green, it represented versatility, animation, and freedom from bondage. There was a metamorphosis going on at that concert which happened every time Garland performed. No wonder she was exhausted. It was like watching a chameleon changing not only its color but its personality.

The last color I saw was blue, the symbol of the spirit. Now that she had the audience's trust, their love, and their complete mental and spiritual attention, the woman onstage was exposing her very soul to them. I have often thought how much more that concert would have meant to me had I understood the meanings of vibrations and colors at that time.

In 1967 when I saw Judy Garland at the Palace Theatre in New York, there wasn't this display of vibratory color around her. In fact, although she was dressed in a bejeweled, glittering pants-suit and was paper-thin, her aura was a dull brownish-gray. The color engulfed her. It was most upsetting, and I would have to look away from the stage and merely listen to her. Now, with some knowledge in the meaning of colors in an aura, I knew that gray, especially the darker tones, symbolizes death. It was the most uncomfortable night I have ever spent in a theater. I knew that Judy Garland would soon be dead.

Every human being has an aura. So does every plant, every living thing, and objects that have been made from living tissue. I also believe that everyone can see auras with but a little bit of assistance.

To find out if you have the ability to "read" auras, try this little experiment: Make the room where you sleep as dark as possible. Have an ordinary magnet at hand. When in bed, relax as much as possible. If you are familiar with meditation, meditate for a short time. Calm, peaceful vibrations are necessary. If the room is not completely dark, take the magnet and slip under the bedcovers. Hold the magnet somewhat away from yourself and gaze in its direction. After some time, you should be able to see a very faint light emanating from both poles of the magnet. According to your ability to distinguish auras, the light from the magnet will be either a very faint glow or an intense, well-defined emanation, or possibly somewhere in between these two extremes. Even if you see nothing, you should repeat this procedure on successive nights. I feel everyone can see auras with practice.

After you have success in this elementary test, you should then go on to developing the ability with another person, or a plant, or any living thing. In the beginning you should make sure that you are harmonious with whatever living thing you have chosen for the test. Do not, for instance, choose someone whom you do not particularly get along with or one who is extremely negative in any way.

Evening is the best time for this particular experiment. A dark, unshiny material should be hung up on a wall. The subject sits fifteen to eighteen inches away from the dark material, directly in front of it. For exactly thirty seconds you should then stare at an uncovered one-hundred-watt electric bulb, about three feet away from it. Immediately following this you must sit, clear your mind completely, and become as passive as you can. Begin to focus your attention on the idea of the aura, of seeing it. Then gaze at your subject. You should see some form of light emanating from the subject's body. If you don't see anything this first time, do not give up. Keep at it. It takes much practice to achieve psychic abilities.

You may or may not be able to distinguish colors at first, but you probably will get mental impressions of the color. We often unconsciously think of people in different shades of various colors. List all of your friends, business acquaintances, and family members on a piece of paper. Concentrate on each of them. Try to think of the color that best fits every name you have put down. Jot the color next to the name.

You will find this quite easy to do. One particular friend brings red to mind, another had always reminded you of blue, and so forth. These colors that you attach to people will often be dominant in their auras, colors that you have unconsciously picked up without trying.

I have gone over some of the meanings of colors in this chapter in regard to Judy Garland. Herewith are some more psychic interpretations of the meanings of colors seen in an aura:

Red is known as the first color. It is the most dominant hue in the color spectrum. Too much red in an aura denotes a materialistic person. Dark red, as in Judy Garland's case, means that the person is going through tremendous emotional upheaval. The cloudy red in an aura indicates a somewhat selfish, materialistic person. A magnetic personality, such as Judy Garland, will usually have red in the aura as the dominant color.

In every red-colored aura there is a tendency toward sensual experience rather than the spiritual or the mental. If black is seen with red in an aura, it indicates an extremely sensual person who is not in control of emotions or animal passions.

Yellow in an aura, especially in the bright gold shades, denotes spirituality in a person. Yellow is the color of meditation, of concentration, and is usually attributed to a deep-thinking person. If the aura is mostly yellow, it will show the presence of intelligence. Yellow represents light. Successful and happy businessmen usually have a yellow aura.

Only one shade of yellow is negative, and that is the muddy, darker tone. When this is sensed in the vibrations of an aura, it tells of a jealous personality, one who possesses a suspicious nature.

Orange in an aura indicates energy and strength. Orange is the color of the sun and is therefore vital, forceful. Those people with an orange in their aura are usually quite overpowering and dominate others around them. Many executive types have orange in their aura. But there is a tendency toward kidney disorders in people who have an orange aura.

Green is the color of growth, and when it is found in an aura it means that the person is reaching out, having learning experiences. It is the color of supply, of regeneration. The more emerald color denotes healing abilities. (It is no accident that hospitals now utilize green or green-blue doctors' and nurses' gowns, or that the walls of many hospital rooms are painted in this color, for it has been proven to have a healing effect on the patients.)

Shades of blue in an aura indicate spirituality. In the Orient, blue-colored objects were placed inside the tombs of the dead to protect their spirits from evil. Those who possess blue auras can be completely trusted, as they are loyal and honest in their relationships. The darker the blue in an aura, the more progressed the person is in spiritual and mental understanding.

The most highly developed people in the realms of spiritual teachings have violet auras. This color has the dominant spirituality of blue mixed with the strength of red. It is of little surprise to find that royalty has always utilized violet in their decorations and dress. They would like their subjects to believe that they are highly evolved, elevated above the rest of the people.

Gray, when in its darker aspect, is the color of death. This sometimes means a spiritual death or even a mental one, wherein the persons expressing this color in their aura are not learning, not taking from their experiences.

If a black aura is indicated, it means a person who is delving, either willingly or unwillingly, into the darker aspects of the occult. I have seen many drug addicts who have black auras, as do alcoholics. It is the color of negation. It is interesting to note that in the Orient, black is never used in any mystical or religious way. It is not seen in the robes of priests or worn even by those who mourn their dead.

With this basic understanding of the colors of vibrations in auras (which science is now proving has validity) the development of being able to sense or see the colors emanating from others is of great value.

Another experiment that can be utilized to see the vibrations of an aura can be done alone or with others. To begin this experiment, you should cover a table with a black cloth, the material having a dull finish. The subject then places the fingertips of both hands together, on the table for at least sixty seconds. The subject then draws the fingers apart very slowly. Vibrations of the aura that emanate from the fingers and unite both hands will be seen.

Experiments with a group can also be most effective. The group should sit around a table covered in black cloth. Everyone then places his hands flat on the table, with the palms down. There should follow a meditation for a short time, not more than twenty-five minutes. One of the group should then lift his hands and point them at the person directly opposite. Vibrations will be seen reaching out to that person. There will be those in the group who will vibrate definite color vibrations; these are the more sensitive, mediumistic individuals. Others will exude a colorless light from their hands. I have seen the auric vibrations of several developed sensitives meet in the center of the table of such a gathering and create what amounted to a thick mist of illumination, like a cloud of light.

You can also develop your awareness of color in aura vibrations. First, the subject should gather three-by-five-inch pieces of different-colored paper, representing each of the primary colors. These bits of paper are then placed in envelopes that cannot be seen through. Sitting in a comfortable chair, the subject then does a meditation or some simple breathing exercises, such as taking long deep breaths, filling the lungs and holding the air for a few seconds as the stomach muscle is pulled in tight, and then slowly exhaling the air until it is all out. This is repeated five to seven times.

As the meditation or breathing exercise is being accomplished, the subject visualizes the primary colors in his mind. The subject then chooses one of the envelopes at random and either places it against the forehead or holds it tight between two hands. With deep concentration, the subject works on "seeing" or sensing the correct color inside the envelope. The subject then writes down the color on a piece of paper. This is done with all the envelopes in turn. With practice, it is amazing how even the most seemingly inept person will eventually be able to distinguish the various colors within the envelope.

As you progress in these simple experiments, you should try to sense the colors in the auras around your acquaintances. This may take months, even years, of practice, or just several days, but there is no doubt that the reading of auras can be accomplished. Sensing the vibrations that emanate from all living things is not allocated just to a gifted few. If one places value on the auric vibrations and works to develop this ability, it can be used in dealing with others on all levels of communication—personal relationships, business dealings, and so on. It is but another step toward the total awareness of one's environment.

Vibrations
of Chance

I returned and saw under the sun, that the race is not to the swift, nor the battle to the strong, neither yet bread to the wise, nor yet riches to men of understanding, nor yet favour to men of skill; but time and chance happeneth to them all.

Ecclesiastes 9:II

Writing about his play *Orphée*, Jean Cocteau recalled that "the night before opening night, we rehearsed in the vestibule of my apartment. [The actor] Herrand had just said the line: 'With these gloves you will pass through mirrors as if they were water,' when there was a tremendous crash at the other end of the apartment. A huge mirror in the bathroom had fallen out of its frame: the shattered fragments covered the floor. . . .

"A year later I was having lunch with [Glenway Wescott and Monroe Wheeler] in their very isolated house on a hillside above Villefranche-sur-Mer. They were translating *Orphée* and told me a glazier would be incomprehensible in America. . . . 'In Paris,' I told them, 'you almost never see one.' They asked me to describe a glazier for them, and were just seeing me to the gate, crossing the garden, when, contrary to all expectation and likelihood, a glazier came walking along the deserted road, then vanished around a bend."

I have never believed in chance happenings. Even as a child, whenever anyone would say to me, "Isn't that a strange coincidence?" I knew that whatever that person was talking about was *not* some idle occurrence.

I believe that the vibrations surrounding each of us often attract similar vibrations into our sphere of being. Incidents that appear to be coincidental are actually like-vibrations, brought into the same action from the energy fields that make up all persons, places, and things.

Edward H. Sothern was a well-known actor in the late 1890s. His personal case of a most dramatic "coincidental" happening is recorded in his autobiography, *My Remembrances*.

Edward's father, Edward A. Sothern, Sr., loved fox hunting and was actually quite good at it. He was often invited on fox hunts by well-known and rich society personages of the day. One such riding companion was the Prince of Wales. After completing several hunts with Edward, Sr., the prince presented him with a gift—a beautiful gold matchbox, personally engraved. It was quite elaborate and one of a kind.

One day while on a hunt, Edward, Sr., fell from his horse. When he picked himself up from the ground, he discovered that the matchbox was gone; somehow it had been torn from the watch chain that it had been attached to. Although he searched diligently for the matchbox, Edward could not find it anywhere. Sothern was most upset about the loss and almost immediately ordered a duplicate of it from the exclusive store where the Prince of Wales had had the original designed and created.

Some years later, Edward's second son, Samuel, was about to depart on a theatrical tour across the ocean in Australia. Edward gave the duplicate to the young man to carry as a good-luck charm. When Samuel was traveling in Australia, he gave the matchbox as a gift to an Australian by the name of Labertouche who had befriended him.

Eventually, Samuel returned to his home in England. He loved fox hunting as much as his father and continued the sport. While riding to the hounds with a bunch of other hunters, an old gentleman-farmer approached Samuel and introduced himself.

"Are you Edward Sothern's son?" the farmer asked.

"Yes" was the reply.

The farmer then told Samuel that just that morning one of his farmhands had dug up the original matchbox belonging to Edward, Sr. It had been buried for over twenty years on his property where it must have been lost.

Samuel was more than a bit shaken by the odd coincidence. It had been the first time that he had met the farmer who had that very morning found his father's golden matchbox. He dashed off a letter to his brother, Edward, Jr., who was also an actor and at that time on a tour of America.

Edward, Jr., received his brother's letter, but did not open it until he was on a train heading toward his next theatrical engagement. He was seated next to another actor, Arthur Lawrence. They had been introduced but a few hours before. Edward read his brother's letter and then related the coincidence of the found matchbox.

"I do wonder whatever happened to the duplicate?" Edward said, thinking aloud.

Arthur Lawrence's face turned ashen. He reached into his vest pocket for his watch chain. From it hung a gift that had been presented to him by a Mr. Labertouche while he was on an acting tour of Australia. It was the duplicate of the golden matchbox! Both men stared at each other in shocked, stunned silence.

The odds of this incident happening are not only highly improbable, but by all intellectual reasoning impossible. The chance of each person and object being brought together are staggering to one's sense of credibility. The matchboxes covered not only three separate continents but two generations as well. In no way can this be labeled mere coincidence.

The energy field that surrounded the matchboxes was linked to the vibrations of the Sothern family through time and space. No matter where they would have traveled, I believe that the original matchbox and its duplicate would eventually have come back into the Sothern family orbit. Vibratory magnetism drew the objects and the family together.

Paul Krammerer was an Austrian biologist who accomplished much in his investigation of coincidental occurrences. Krammerer set up a theory that he called "seriality," outlined in his book *The Law of the Series* (1919). In this excellent work, Krammerer wrote, "We thus arrive at the image of a world—mosaic or cosmic kaleidoscope, which, in spite of constant shufflings and rearrangements, also takes care of bringing like and like together."

At the age of twenty, Krammerer started to keep a record of "coincidences" and continued doing so for two decades. He carefully numbered and systemized the hundreds of examples of "chance happenings" that he was to discover. From mathematical tables, Krammerer proved that the cycles and series of coincidences broke all the laws of probability, falling together in their own transcendent patterns. "Certain random events," Krammerer deducted, "are not fractures in the great chain of cause and effect—rather, they respond to the tug of another order entirely."

Carl Jung, a contemporary of Krammerer, also believed that coincidences weren't to be looked at from the point of view as mere chance happenings. Jung kept his own record of odd "coincidences" and strange occurrences. The French astronomer Camille Flammarion (1842-1925) related the following to Jung, which Flammarion had authenticated as being true.

Monsieur Deschamps was born in Orléans, France. In his youth, Deschamps was given his initial taste of plum pudding by a certain Monsieur de

Fortgibu. Deschamps loved it, and more than ten years later, while in a French restaurant he had not been in before, he ordered a dish of the dessert.

"I am truly sorry, monsieur," the waiter explained, "but another gentleman had just ordered the last portion. May I suggest something else?"

Deschamps turned to the table where the last portion of plum pudding was headed. To his complete surpirse, Deschamps saw that the man who had ordered the last of the pudding was the same de Fortgibu who a decade earlier had introduced him to the taste of the fruit dessert, and whom he had not seen since.

Years later, while at a dinner party he was attending, Deschamps was served plum pudding. He regaled the other guests with his story of the odd coincidence of the plum pudding and de Fortgibu. They all agreed that it was strange that Deschamps should have ordered the pudding in the restaurant where de Fortgibu had just put in his order for the last serving.

Suddenly, the door to the party was thrust open. An elderly, much confused man stepped into the room. He immediately looked quite embarrassed. He had obtained an incorrect address and had arrived at this house by complete mistake, expecting to find some friends with whom he was going to have dinner. The man was the very same de Fortgibu!

Paul Krammerer felt that there might have been some unknown, physical cause or explanation for the coincidence. On the other hand, Carl Jung believed that some psychic force had been the motivating factor. "It is the unconscious mind," Jung declared, "a place where cause and effect have no meaning; the unconscious mind where space and time actually disappear. Coincidences are merely the outward expressions of this paraphysical order of things. They appear in answer to any deeper vibratory symbol that may be sent out."

In this instance, the pudding (or the desire for it) acted as the trigger for the so-called coincidence. The vibrations of both these men were somehow linked and brought together by their common attraction to a certain food. Or was it more urgent than that? Were not these men brought together for some other reason that neither of them explored?

Jung often related a coincidence that helped him to cure a woman patient. The young woman, deep in therapy with Jung, told him of a particular dream she had been having. In this dream, someone had presented her with a golden scarab. At the instant she was relating her dream to Jung, there was a tapping sound at the windowpane. A bug was banging itself against the glass, as though it desired access into the darkened room (there was no light in the room to attract it). Jung opened the window and caught the insect—it was a scarab beetle!

"Here's your scarab," he said to his shocked patient.

This extraordinary coincidence of a dream and

its eventual reality was instrumental in opening up a new avenue of therapy for the woman. Previously she had experienced much anxiety over her treatment. Jung theorized that her deep-rooted anxiety had somehow triggered her unconscious to react by affording a glimpse of the future in a dream state of consciousness.

Jung wrote that this case had been extremely difficult, almost impossible to treat, and that, "up to the time of the dream, little or no progress had been made. I should explain that the main reason for this was my patient's animus, which was steeped in Cartesian philosophy and clung so rigidly to its own idea of reality that the efforts of three doctors [Jung was the third to treat the unfortunate woman] had not been able to weaken it. Evidently, something quite irrational was needed which was beyond my powers to produce."

On another level, Jung realized that the scarab is a classic symbol of rebirth. Thus, the insect became symbolic of the woman's reemergence; her cure was responsible for the creation of a "new person." When one accepts the theory of "seriality" as put forth by Paul Krammerer, both the beetle and the matchbox stories of coincidence become far less sensational.

A few years ago, a friend of mine and I had been having difficulty regarding several personal matters. We had been very close. We decided to go for a walk and talk things over. This friend had been having a strong urge to end our relationship, and I had been coming to that same conclusion myself. It was a traumatic time for both of us.

Strolling down a busy New York City street, he spotted something shiny on the sidewalk. Although many people were hurrying by, no one else seemed to take note of the small object. My friend reached down and picked it up. It was a silver ring, half of which was carved with a single geometric design. On the other half, carved in clear, block form, were the letters D.L. We could not believe it. The possibility of finding a ring with my initials on it is, of course, not impossible, but quite remote. The odds of discovering the ring at a time when my friend had taken this walk to mull over the continuation of our relationship is high. That the ring fit my finger perfectly (I have unusually small hands) makes the odds more improbable.

On a much deeper level of awareness, rings are symbolic of a union, of friendship. The ring became a symbol to me that the karma my friend and I had was not over, that we were to continue as friends. We became much closer after this incident. I think that the omen of the ring startled us into a new level of awareness that we had not had before.

Joyce Orser, an astrologist friend of mine, is the cofounder of Star, an organization located in Poughkeepsie, New York. Star is devoted to assisting people through various forms of awareness, from astrology to meditation to graphology. While I was in the midst of doing this chapter, Joyce came to my house for a visit. We had a most interesting talk about the occult, and I began telling her some of the stories of coincidence that I had been uncovering. She was particularly intrigued with the account of Jung and the beetle.

"This fascinates me," Joyce said. Her thick dark hair that framed her exquisite Egyptian-like features bobbed up and down as she shook her head in wonderment. "There is so much that goes on in our world that we know so little about. I haven't given thought to coincidence in regards to the paranormal, but I certainly will be on guard for such occurrences."

A day later, Joyce called me. "Gee, you know, I had an interesting experience that I know relates in some way to our conversation yesterday." It was very warm when she left my house. The temperature was so high that she decided to stop off at the Howard Johnson's on her way home and get a dish of her favorite ice cream. As she sat at the counter, a man sitting across from her exclaimed in a rather loud voice, "Well, I'll be damned! Isn't this something?" looking down at the napkin on his lap.

Joyce glanced down and saw that a large green inchworm was crawling on his napkin. "You probably brought it in with you on your clothes from outside," she offered an explanation.

He shook his head. "You know what? This is the third green inchworm that I have found on a napkin in three different restaurants in the past month!"

Joyce felt a chill go over her body. It was just what we had been talking about. The odds of this man finding three inchworms on three napkins in three different restaurants in three different sections is quite remote.

Why inchworms? Joyce thought. And why in restaurants, always on his napkin? She had no answer, but felt that if the man was to tune in, he would probably come up with some reason or explanation.

"Maybe the inchworms were waiting for you, knew you were coming." Joyce smiled at her own response. The man stared at her as though she were odd.

Arriving home, Joyce pondered over the theories of coincidence and recalled another happening in her life that was "coincidental." Years ago, she had been talking with an acquaintance who informed Joyce that he had just got a spider monkey as a pet. Animals are one of Joyce's interests and they had a long conversation about the new pet. She was very surprised to learn that this particular species of monkey is very small.

Later in the day as she was driving on the highway headed for home, Joyce began to think about the spider monkey again. It had amazed her that the animals were so small. She was in the right lane and came up to a car going rather slowly. Joyce decided to pass the car. As she did, something made her glance over at the driver of the other car. On the man's shoulder was a small animal. Joyce looked again out of disbelief. It was a spider monkey.

The incident so unglued her that she had to strain to keep the car on the road. To be thinking of something that she had never seen before in her life and to be confronted with it at that instant was unnerving to say the least.

If we keep our eyes open and our senses tuned, we would discover many coincidences in our lives that bear investigation. Some will appear incidental, and others could have direct bearing on our lives and soul progress. Coincidences should not be shrugged off as chance but carefully scrutinized to find what need or action *created* the coincidence.

In recent studies at Duke University's Institute for Parapsychology, it was discovered that vibratory fields of energy extend to the lower forms of animal life as well the higher. This, too, brought into play the question of coincidence.

One experiment at Duke is particularly revealing. Baby chickens were placed under a heat lamp that was switched on, then off via a hyper-random process, according to the discharge of elementary particles from radioactive materials. A computerized calculator added up the number of times the lamp was either lit or turned off. When the chicks had the heat from the lamp, they expressed contentment and were relaxed, showing every sign of complete enjoyment. When the lamp was turned off, the chicks huddled close together and chirped miserably.

The automatic overhead light hovered over "her brood" for many days and was lit far more often than not. But when the chicks were removed from beneath the lamp, it turned itself on less than half the time it did when the chicks had lived beneath it!

Questions naturally arose. Did the chicks' need for light create a vibratory force that reached upward and turned the light on more often than not? Were the chicks able to create some sort of psychokinesis through their need for warmth, strong enough to bend chance and turn the automatic light switch on? One thing was certain—the possibility of coincidence was eliminated, for the odds of the switch turning on more often when the chicks were beneath it is beyond all chance.

As I am writing this, I have come across headlines in New York newspapers that tell of a most unusual series of coincidences. In a forty-eight-hour period during the first week of July 1975, thirty-five persons met violent deaths in New York City. According to the city's medical examiner, Dr. Dominick Di Maio, it was an "astonishingly high number. Never in my experience have I seen so many violent, unrelated deaths. And I have been with the medical examiner's office since 1947."

An even stranger aspect of the "two days of death" was the fact that more than a quarter of the victims died in plunges from buildings. Di Maio said that there was "no scientific explanation of why this should have happened. Nothing links these people together. There is no apparent reason so many deaths should have happened on those two particular days."

In any large city, the summer months are conducive to an atmosphere where violence can erupt. People are on the streets later at night, they drink more, and tempers flare much more than in cooler weather. However, on both these days the weather was *cooler* than usual, with a temperature range of 66° to 80° (the normal temperature for that time of the month is 85°).

Interestingly, Di Maio shrugged off the death period by saying, "Though murder and suicide are sometimes linked together, there's nothing to link them with those two particular days . . . unless maybe you believe in astrology."

Maybe he wasn't too far from the truth with that supercilious remark. When there is no other explanation for chance occurrences, relating the unnatural happening to the occult usually gets a big laugh. It is my belief that many people pick up on the vibrations that permeate the atmosphere and react accordingly. For some reason, the vibrations of death were strong in New York City on those two days in question. Many people not only sensed the negative energy surrounding them but allowed this energy to enter their own vibratory field, becoming a part of it and then committing negative actions.

Exactly one week later, negative vibrations ran rampant in southern California. In a two-day period many persons were murdered, including two semi-well-known TV actors who were shot down in cold blood as they left a yoga class in Hollywood. Were these two days of death in California also a coincidence? More likely it was the negative energy that flowed through the streets that people picked up on and utilized.

If one was to take note of the sequence of plane crashes, it would be substantiated that such accidents do come in series. There are long periods when no crashes take place, and then suddenly several will occur in a short duration of time. For example, the crash of a jet at Kennedy Airport in New York was soon followed by the crash of a similar plane in Morocco. The accidents took the lives of hundreds of victims. Following the newspapers, you will find that there is almost a pattern of plane crashes that follow one another in some form of sequence.

Coincidence? Did the pilots become receivers of the negative vibrations? Or did the passengers on a second or third plane conjure up such fear in their minds when they heard of the first plane that they themselves attracted the negative vibrations to the plane? When I get on a plane, I try to sense the vibrations of the other passengers. If ever I got a general negative feeling that predominated from them, I would get off the plane.

As your own awareness grows, you become capable of correctly sensing other vibrations in places and situations. You become able to translate for your benefit what you unconsciously pick up about other people, new areas, and prospective homes. Sometimes it will be the vibrations of those who have been in a place before you; often, you can sense the real good emanating from a person or a place, and of course, negativity when that is being sent out.

With Malice
Aforethought

I do not believe that "ghosts" are responsible for what occurred on Gene's farmland or what happened to those who dared to break into the sacred burial tombs of Egypt. The energy that was created remains in these areas. It does not dissipate and can be most negative to those who attempt to tamper with what the energy was meant to protect.

It would be very wise for America to begin work on the investigation of how vibratory levels of energy can be created and put to use. The Russians are well into it, and there is talk that China is also involved in mind power or energy. Thousands of people concentrating their psychic energies in a certain direction can indeed change the weather or bring about other positive effects.

When I had the opportunity to travel with the American Indians and see how they lived, I began to realize that much of the ritual in which they involved themselves is actually the creation of a vibratory level, the bringing up of an energy. This is what a rain dance is. Indians will begin the dance while praying for the rain to come, sending out a mass energy. It is not the music or the dancing that brings rain, but the concentrated effort placed into the atmosphere by many people directing their thoughts in that direction. And it does work, no question. Right in the midst of a drought, after one of these tribal rituals, I have seen it pour.

In some Buddhist sects, a person repeats a certain desire or wish over and over again into the air—hundreds, maybe thousands, of times. By doing this, the sheer force of the concentrated physical effort of the repitition creates an energy. The Buddhist is taught to "put his entire emotional being" into this "chanting" for something. His energy can (and often is) completely spent in the repeating of his desire. The creation of these energies or vibrations is most effective, as I have seen this technique in action.

Catholics repeat endless prayers (such as saying the rosary beads over and over) for the sick, or for something they desire. When the person concentrates his emotions into these prayers, an energy is created that can set the need into reality.

However, I have always believed in the ancient saying "Be careful what you pray for, eventually you will get it." If you work for something with great concentrations of energy, it will happen—but maybe not the way you wanted it to.

When prayers are not answered, the energy level was not sufficiently built up; the prayers were merely lip service and not committed with any emotional outpouring. This is the basis of the short story "The Monkey's Paw." When the family is granted three wishes, they set up such an emotional fervor for the return of their dead son that the lad does come back, albeit from the grave and looking the same way he did when he died falling into a threshing machine.

There are individuals and groups that certainly can send out negative vibrations. In a previous book, *America Bewitched* (William Morrow, 1973), I went into depth about the vibrations of negation. The Satan worshipers use the vibrations of error, negation, low emotions, for their own benefit. And there is proof that these negative vibrations can do *much* damage. I would like to include at least one documented example of their effectiveness. This particular happening is a part of the history of the area where I live. It has been written about by many historians and was recently included in Alf Evers' magnificent history *The Catskills: From Wilderness to Woodstock* (Doubleday, 1972).

Following the American Revolution, the Catskill Mountain area was opened up to vast numbers of settlers. Among them were persons with various forms of psychic abilities who seemed to be attracted to the magnificent natural beauty of the then mostly uncharted wilderness.

Many of those who utilized psychic talents were of German and English descent, people who had escaped persecution of the infamous European witch hunts. The only reason that they were not persecuted in New York, as many were in Salem, was that the Dutch who ruled New Amsterdam and environs had a very open mind toward unorthodox religious beliefs. The Dutch had brought their tolerance and fairness toward all forms of religious sects—and witches—with them from Holland. Thus the witches and conjurers of the Hudson Valley were permitted to work their powers, but only if they were subject to the countermeasures of what were termed "witch doctors" or "white doctors." These people were said to have the power to nullify and render harmless any kinds of spells or curses that the witches had created.

Naturally, myths sprung up around this area and it is sometimes impossible to separate the legend from the truth. There were also those persons who were eager for attention and would bring notoriety unto themselves by acting the way witches were supposed to act. This would usually gain them the feared respect of their neighbors. On the other hand, there were happenings that were of a definite psychic nature and could not be explained as hoax.

The most famous witch doctor was one Jacob Brink. He was a seventh son of a seventh son, and therefore it was believed that he was most fitted to do this kind of work.

Jacob Brink had healing ability. One of the mysterious talents that he possessed was a proficiency in stopping the flow of blood. This talent worked with animals as well as humans.

One documented story tells of a man who came to the Brink home in desperation. His horse had been somehow cut and the animal was bleeding to death. Brink threw back his head and went into a trancelike state that lasted for several minutes. When he emerged from the altered state of consciousness, Brink looked at the man and said. "Go home. The bleeding has stopped." When the man arrived at his house, he found that the horse's bleeding had indeed ceased.

There were other renowned "white witches." Dr. E. H. Benjamin was a forerunner of Edgar Cayce and operated in much the same manner, giving diagnoses and prescribing for people who were ill while he was in the state of deep trance.

The most documented and researched occurrence of this time involved Jacob Brink and the famous "haunted sloop of the Hudson." In 1820 a wealthy merchant by the name of Abraham Hasbrouck was living at the base of the Catskills in the town of Roundout, right alongside the Hudson River. Sloops then carried goods up and down the Hudson from the smaller towns and settlements to New York City and back. Hasbrouck decided that he was going to build the fastest sloop on the river and his ship, to be called the *Martin Wyncoop*, was designed for that purpose.

In the midst of building the vessel, Hasbrouck's trouble began. An old woman who was a practicing witch in the region entered Hasbrouck's goods store and inquired about a particular brand of snuff that she used. Hasbrouck told her that he did not carry the particular brand, but that it could be ordered for her. He said that he would get her some and that it would be in the store on a subsequent visit. The woman left. Hasbrouck promptly forgot about the snuff and did not order it.

A week or so passed. The old woman returned to Hasbrouck's store, whereupon she was informed that the order for her snuff had been neglected. She became infuriated and said that she was going to put a curse on the vessel he was building; she was going to place bad vibrations around it. With that, the old woman left the store, vowing to keep her promise.

From that instant, everything went wrong with the *Martin Wyncoop*. Several men working on the ship were seriously injured. Completed work on the boat was discovered to be wanting and had to be ripped out and done over. Uncommon flaws were found in the materials being used on the sloop and had to be replaced.

Finally, the *Martin Wyncoop* was ready for launching. All the wood and moorings that had held her back from the water as she was being made ready were removed. The ways had been greased. But the *Martin Wyncoop* did not slide down from its stocks. It remained on the ways, not moving an inch. The ship was pushed, pulled, and shook in attempts to make it move. Nothing.

Hasbrouck, who by now was believing that the witch had indeed put a curse on his boat, called in the "witch doctor." When Jacob Brink arrived, he immediately began to recite some incantations meant to nullify the curse, to change the vibrations from negative to positive. The boat responded and rushed headlong into the water.

But the apparent vibratory force that the witch had placed around the sloop was not displaced for long. On one of the boat's first trips to New York City, Hasbrouck's son fell down the hold, broke his neck, and died instantly. On another trip the boat capsized for no apparent reason. All the valuable cargo that was on board was lost and the boat's cook drowned.

Not one year passed without members of the crew coming away from their trips with broken arms, legs, or other injuries. On one occasion the sloop rammed into a ship called the *Constitution* and both of them almost sank. The *Martin Wyncoop* did sink on several trips to New York City and had to be lifted up from the murky depth of the Hudson each time.

The crews that boarded the *Martin Wyncoop* would never stay with the ship for long periods of time. They would sign on one season and then sign off the next. They said that in addition to the unusual number of physical disasters encountered on the relatively short and easy trip to New York City, there were other things to contend with. At night, moored on the river, members of the crew would be awakened by the sound of walking on the deck. Often, the splash of an anchor being dropped overboard would awaken them. When they would investigate, invariably there would be nothing on deck. These noises were at first attributed to the large number of rats that had made their homes on the boat, but even after these vermin were eliminated, the noises continued.

The most unusual of all the occurrences concerning the *Martin Wyncoop* happened on a summer day when the sloop had just left its mooring place from the town of Catskill and was about to head downriver for New York. It had been one of those glorious summer days; the sun shone bright in the blue sky. There was a strong wind. The river was flowing steadily.

The sloop had left the docks and was about to embark for its destination when it came to an abrupt halt. The anchor was checked. It was up. Perhaps one or two of the ropes that had held the boat to its mooring place had not been untied? No, all of the ropes had been made secure on the ship. Well, the captain rationalized, she must have run aground. This was checked. The boat was found not to be resting on anything but water. The vessel acted as though it had been frozen in the water as it had been many times during a winter's day on the icy Hudson.

The captain realized that this had to be the work of the witch who had placed evil vibrations around the boat. As a last resort, Jacob Brink was called to the scene. Brink arrived and came onboard with a "witch's whip." He opened his book of white magic rituals that he often brought with him on these tasks and began whipping the decks of the ship from stem to stern. As he did this, Brink read some of the prayers from his book. There was said to have been the sound of plopping in the water, like objects or persons falling or jumping over the side of the railing. As Brink came to the completion of his work, the ship shook, became free from whatever it was that had held it so fast, and bounded forward. It then continued on its way.

The boat changed hands many times, because those who owned it would go bankrupt or be stricken by some personal disaster. Finally, in 1889, with a heavy load of bricks on board, the *Martin Wyncoop* sank to the bottom of the North River just off Brimstone Point on the New Jersey shore. Its current owners had just purchased the sloop and this had been her initial trip for them. They decided to make no attempt to salvage the boat. To this day the *Martin Wyncoop* lies in that stretch of water.

As in the case of the sending of positive vibrations for healing, the same energy can be used for negative purposes with just as much an effect. Groups of people, on a large scale, can create much harm by the utilization of such vibrations. I feel that future wars will certainly utilize aspects of mind energy against opponents. And indeed, many countries are now involved in experiments for this very purpose.

9

Healing

The sending of vibrations to others does work. The exact opposite of a curse is healing. The energy is the same, but the thought and motivation is positive rather than destructive. It can be just as effective, since vibrations can build as well as tear down.

V.: Once I had this flowering plant given to me that I didn't like. It didn't grow well; in fact it did very poorly. Its leaves kept drooping and turning brown. One day I decided to experiment. I physically sat down next to the plant and told it to forgive me and that I did love it. Eventually it did grow, but it took six months to convince this plant.

Another time I was given a purple passion plant. The person who gave it to me said that this particular plant never blossomed and that passion plants seldom do. Well, I talked to that plant every day, expressing love toward it. It has grown tremendously and is now in blossom, and I mean loaded with buds. The plant picked up my vibrations, my feelings toward it. The first plant took six months to respond, for it somehow picked up the truth: that I did not like it. My vibrations were not real.

Logan: Then you believe that it isn't only mankind that gives off vibrations?

V.: Plants do, animals do. I have this cat Yo-Yo, a Siamese. Whenever I am not feeling well or am upset, this cat will do anything to get near me. She even will get into bed with me. I feel better almost instantly. She senses my feelings and gives off her own positive vibes. She responds to me with love, and I do feel better.

Logan: I know what you mean. I have a cat that knows when I am sick and will get close to a particular area, such as my stomach when that is out of whack, and start kneading it. . . .

The cramp in my leg had come back. I was truly in pain. There was no sense in going on.

"Eileen," I turned and said to my secretary and present traveling companion, "I've got to pull over. I hurt so bad that if I don't stop driving and get off this highway immediately I'm afraid we might have an accident."

"Okay," Eileen said in a matter-of-fact tone. "We've got to get back to New York City by this evening. You're always telling me that I have healing abilities. Let's see if I can work it for you."

Eileen had accompanied me on a successful lecture for a Spiritual Frontiers Fellowship group in northern New York State and we were returning home when the leg cramps struck. Over the past several months, I had been experiencing these cramps whenever taking automobile trips of any duration. The cramp would set in behind the right knee, where the leg bends. The leg would buckle from beneath me, the pain was that excruciating.

Eileen and I managed to get off the highway and onto a rest-picnic area. The pain was so intense and unbearable I had to have help getting out of the car.

With Eileen's assistance, I stumbled over to a redwood table and bench. I perched myself atop the table and held the leg straight out, as I could no longer bend it without almost blacking out.

I rolled up my pants leg. Eileen sat on the bench alongside me. She placed both hands around the afflicted area. The pain had become excruciating and I flinched at her slightest touch. She withdrew her hands instantly.

"It's okay," I said to her. "It'll hurt at first, but please try. I want you to try to heal it, otherwise we'll be searching for a doctor. The way I'm feeling, we're not going anywhere!"

Eileen once again put her hands on my agonizingly painful leg. She closed her eyes and bade me to do the same. Then Eileen asked me to try to relax. She felt the tension caused by pain that had caused me to stiffen my entire body. I attempted to relax, with much difficulty under the circumstance.

Eileen did not move her hands over the painful area as some healers would have done. She simply held her hands in place. It was autumn and her hands were cold when she first touched me, but within a few seconds the coldness completely abated. I began to feel a warm sensation emanating from Eileen's hands. Another moment passed and the warmth was replaced by a sensation of radiating heat.

"Your hands feel like a heating pad that has been turned up on high!" I exclaimed. "I've never felt such a strong sensation of heat coming from anyone before."

Eileen didn't respond. Her eyes were closed.

Several more moments passed. I began to feel a definite movement in her hands, pulsating, rhythm-like. I looked to see if Eileen was moving her hands in any physical way. She wasn't. I then began to feel short needlelike pricks on the surface of the skin beneath Eileen's hands. It was a bit uncomfortable. I watched the procedure quite carefully. Eileen was not moving or manipulating her hands in any way, but the vibrations of hot tingling continued to come from her.

Five minutes passed since the healing had started. I felt a sudden twitching in the leg muscle. A flow of energy from Eileen's hands into the muscle was evident.

After about fifteen minutes, Eileen opened her eyes and asked me how I felt. She slowly removed her hands and forceably shook her fingers, as though her hands were wet and she was throwing off water. I told Eileen that I could still feel heat around the afflicted area, as if her hands had not been removed. Carefully, I bent the leg. There seemed to be much less pain.

I got off the table and walked around it. The pain was about 80 percent gone. We were able to get into the car and drive on to our original destination. Before leaving for my own apartment, Eileen gave me one more healing.

A week later I asked Eileen for another healing on the leg; there was still some pain. She acquiesced. It was the last time that I have had a problem with that leg, although I drive much more than before and for longer periods of time. In fact, the problem was nowhere evident during a long drive from New York to Florida and back.

Since that time, I have asked Eileen to work on various physical conditions that have sprung up—headaches, muscle strains, lower back pain, even a severe stomach condition. The pain was always made less. I wasn't always *healed* by Eileen's healing touch, but there was always improvement.

One evening, while administering a healing to me, I glanced over at Eileen's hands and saw an interesting phenomenon—her hands were giving off little sparks, kind of like the sparklers set off on the Fourth of July, although not as bright nor far extending. The energy she creates while healing can be seen as well as felt.

I asked Eileen what it is that she experiences while giving healings.

"Well," Eileen responded, "I feel this vibration force as well as the person I am working on can feel it. It has always amazed me that my hands can act so involuntary of myself. They do become warm, almost hot, and they do vibrate. I have no control over this, however. I merely concentrate on the part of the body I am touching and I try to see it as healed at the same time I am laying my hands on the afflicted section of the anatomy. The vibrations continue after I lift my hands from the person I am working on, and usually I have to physically shake my hands to make them stop vibrating. I am not a professional healer, nor do

I have patients. I do it for family or friends who can accept it. I didn't even know that I had any healing ability until it was pointed out to me only a few years ago by a psychic. I still don't know exactly what happens, but I do know that it works. And if I can help someone, relieve some pain even for a short duration, then why not?"

Dr. Stanley Krippner is a scientist who is devoting a major part of his life's work to the study of parapsychology. He is vice-president of the International Association for Psychotronic Research. He is also the president of the Association for Humanistic Psychology. Dr. Krippner has both a master's and a doctorate in special education.

Dr. Krippner recently stated that it wouldn't be stretching his imagination very much to believe that there are electrical fields around the hands of some people. He says that this energy field enables them to do very extraordinary things, in the manner that a laser beam does. Dr. Krippner says it has been proven that bones heal more quickly when treated with electrical therapy. Even the leg of a salamander can be regenerated more rapidly when it is electrically stimulated.

"It is probable," Dr. Krippner has said, "that there are electrical fields that some people are able to produce voluntarily when they work with sick individuals."

Eileen Dent gives off some sort of electrical vibrational energy when she is healing.

One other such person who has demonstrated

this strong electrical field is Dean Kraft, a young man who was born and raised in Brooklyn. In a very short span of time, Kraft has treated over two hundred people and has proven an uncanny ability to not only alleviate very painful conditions but reverse the diagnosis of medically incurable, untreatable illnesses in those who seek him out.

It is most refreshing to find such a young man going into the science of psychic healing instead of utilizing this energy for sensational show, such as bending spoons and keys. Kraft also does not have the sickening pretentiousness of some faith healers whose zealous "you-can-be-healed-only-through-Christ" attitude should be enough to turn off anyone with even a smattering of intelligence. Most of the population of the world is not Christian, and many non-Christian religions practice forms of spiritual or psychic healing.

Dean Kraft is Jewish. He has no pretensions of grandeur, no feeling that a "divine force" is utilizing him. He simply has an ability to heal and uses it as best he can. He does not tell people that they must believe in this holy being or that; although I do suspect that (as in the case with most psychically gifted people) Kraft has a deeper relationship with a higher, more spiritual source of energy than most.

Kraft has demonstrated his psychic abilities on many occasions and there is no question that what he possesses is the ability to give off energy, or vibrations, that can heal and do other paranormal things. At one established testing institute there is a pendulum suspended in a glass cage. Dozens of wires connect this pendulum to some very delicate sensors which can feel the slightest interference, any kind of magnetism or even radiation. A laser beam is aimed at the pendulum's blade, and any change or movements that occur are recorded on a graph.

Many of the occult's leading practitioners have attempted to make the pendulum move through psychokinesis. Each has failed. But in his first attempt to mentally generate psychic energy to move the pendulum, Kraft made it shake. The next day he knocked the shaft off its treadle by concentrating his vibrations toward it.

Since then, Kraft has successfully proven his psychokinetic and healing abilities before many scientists, doctors, and general researchers. The government has become interested in him and is setting up programs that will further test Kraft's talents.

Brian Van Der Horst has written the most objective interview/article on Kraft yet published (*The Village Voice*, December 23, 1974). Van Der Horst appeared neither a follower nor a skeptic in regards to Kraft and his story.

During one interview session, Van Der Horst complained of having the flu. "Why don't you take a crack at me?" he asked Kraft.

Kraft obliged. The blinds were closed and the

room darkened. Van Der Horst sat in an armchair. Kraft was directly in front of him.

"What do I do?" Van Der Horst inquired.

"I want you to just think of pleasant things," Kraft replied.

Van Der Horst said that he closed his eyes and thought about skiing in the Colorado mountains, one of his favorite sport activities. He did peek through half-shut eyes, however, and noticed that Kraft had begun some form of deep breathing.

"His hands were trembling at an enormous rate," Van Der Horst stated. Kraft started passing his hands just above the writer's head and shoulders, occasionally touching these parts of his body. This lasted for some ten minutes. When the "healing" was over, Van Der Horst said that he felt extremely calm and at peace with himself, although a bit light-headed and somewhat elated. After the healing, his cough had entirely stopped.

Van Der Horst was to note that this simple technique was the same administered to four other people who had come to Kraft for treatments. When questioned as to how he accomplishes his work, Kraft said that it was all very intuitive. He simply shuts his eyes and blanks his mind of everything. He says that it feels as though he is at the dentist and is being given gas. "It feels like my whole head is going down, like I don't have a body. It's one whole feeling like your mind is on the top-level floor of a building and it has to go down, six, seven, eight floors, and so on."

This done, Kraft says that he is then able to pinpoint whatever illness or pain there might be in a person. There is an unconscious need for him to help, and he starts to imagine the person perfect in mind and body. "I try to project a good feeling to the person, to actually love them and to bring up their energy level." The last part of the statement is the most important, for this is exactly what he is doing.

When asked if he always touches the same spot when healing, Kraft replies that he does "just what feels right each time." Once he had been most surprised when coming across an acupuncture chart, for he had been using many of the same parts of the body in his own healing technique.

Kraft has the ability to give off his own vibrations to the sick person who, more often than not, will respond by accepting the energy being administered. Kraft has been asked what he himself feels during a healing process. He answers that it is a feeling of warmth, but with chills, "like when you see a movie that warms your heart, it gives you goose pimples."

Kraft demonstrated his P.K. ability to Van Der Horst in his apartment one day. He placed a pen on the shag rug in the living room. Then Kraft hunched over the pen, spread his hands over it, palms down, and did a heavy breathing exercise. Being somewhat skeptical, Van Der Horst bent down and checked the pen—nothing was attached to it. Kraft then made circles over the pen with both hands, and as he did this, he began to hyperventilate. His concentration was so very intense that he proceeded to tremble.

As Kraft moved away from the pen, it began inching through the tufts of the rug toward him. It actually followed him for more than twelve inches. Suddenly, Kraft fell over in an unconscious, semitrancelike state. Van Der Horst immediately picked up the pen and examined it. The pen was made of plastic; there was no metal on it. Therefore, any kind of magnetism was ruled out. There weren't any strings and nothing beneath the rug had pulled it along. Van Der Horst was convinced that the pen had responded to Kraft's energy level. He had created vibrations that set the pen into motion.

When Kraft came out of his unconscious state, he asked for a glass of water.

When Van Der Horst asked what he had experienced, Kraft replied that his eyes were open but out of focus. He said that he also experienced a feeling of complete weightlessness. Kraft says that he "sees the object I want to move as an extension of my own body. So, when I move myself, the object is a part of me and it has to follow." He relates it to walking on a tightrope: "if I lose concentration for even a second, I have to start all over again." When Dr. Jerry Jampolsky of the Child Center Annex in California tested Kraft, he found that the young healer had "more alpha rhythms than you would expect."

Kraft realizes that these "feats" are merely the sensational aspects of his abilities. He is much more interested in the healing work that he has accomplished.

It was in 1972 that Dean Kraft first discovered his abilities in the realms of utilizing his vibratory energies. He was driving home from work with his boss, Buddy Geier, who owned a music shop in Manhattan. It was in November. As they rode along on the highway, the electric door locks on the car started to click and lock themselves. Both men checked to see which was trying to fool the other. But neither of their hands were even near the lock switches. They decided that it was most probably a short in the car's electrical system.

"If there is a spirit in this car," Kraft said jokingly, " give me five clicks."

There was an immediate response of five clicks. Then Kraft asked for ten clicks. Again the requested response. "Fifteen?" That many clicks followed.

"How much is two and two?"

Four clicks were returned. Both men then asked other mathematical questions and the correct answers were always given via the clicking of the door locks.

For more than a year, the two men continued this "game" whenever they were in the automobile. They devised an answer system—two clicks for "yes," one for "no." They started by asking questions they already knew the answers to—questions about work, friends, family. The clicks were always correct.

At the end of 1972, Kraft and Geier devised a second system. The alphabet was slowly spoken aloud and a click would be heard on a certain letter. That letter was written down. The alphabet was started again and recited until a click was heard. This way, not only words but entire sentences were eventually spelled out.

Friends were invited to be in the car and the clicking still continued answering. One day while at work in Geier's store, a crash was heard. Kraft ran out of the shop and found that a woman had been pinned beneath her car in an accident. He and several others helped the woman get out from under the automobile. As she awaited the ambulance, Kraft lifted her head and held it in his arms.

That same night, on the way home from work, the clicks in the car related this message: "Dean, your hand healed today. Help those in need. Dean, you will have many powers. Use them carefully."

Kraft phoned the hospital where the woman had been taken after the accident the day before. He was informed that she had been released. After this, many happenings of a psychic nature began to take place in Kraft's life. At accident sites, he was constantly the first on hand. When he was eating in a local restaurant one day, tables began to move. He found lost articles for friends and relatives. He had congnitive visions, and his forebodings of future events would see fruition.

It was after these events that Kraft seriously began his healing work. There are many proven records of his ability. Pauline Sheinis had been a complete invalid after suffering several strokes more than five years before she came to Kraft. In three to four months of healing sessions, she was able to regain use of the upper part of her body. Her fearful and constant pain had been considerably reduced.

A New York family-court judge (who wishes to remain anonymous) had an incurable arthritic condition in his back and legs over a period of years. After some healing sessions with Kraft, the "pains left me and I haven't had any problems since."

The list goes on: A woman afflicted with shingles for more than two months was completely healed. Headaches, inner ear disorders, kidney stones, skin diseases, strokes, and even the dreaded cancer have all responded to Kraft's healing vibrations.

There has been some backlash regarding the clicks and the other phenomena. One day when Kraft and Geier asked what was the name of the one doing the clicking, the lock clicking spelled out the word "God." Both men got upset. "Why us?" they naturally asked. The clicks spelled out that they were "chosen." Other religious messages from the clicking spoke of Dean Kraft as some kind of messiah.

When asked what he thinks of the messages' religious connotations, Kraft would usually say, "Blaah. I don't know, it all sounds so nutty. I'm just trying to find out what it is that I'm doing through healing. I try not to think of the rest."

Van Der Horst asked Kraft it he could have been making the locks click psychokinetically by his own subconscious. Kraft said that it took a lot of concentration to move them and that he couldn't do any P.K. stuff at that time. He had not even tried it before. He feels that the clicking serves merely as a stepping-stone to his healing activities. He doesn't care if it was his subconscious, something supernatural, or even a communication from a source beyond. "If it's a step to helping people, I don't care. It's getting there that counts."

Former astronaut Ed Mitchell feels that the publicity Kraft is getting is destructive. "I've seen it happen so many times that it appalls me," Mitchell told Brian Van Der Horst in an interview. "Every decent psychic we start to work with eventually gets grabbed hold of by the press and blown up into an egomaniac, totally worthless to anyone, including himself. There are thousands of people in this country who can do whatever he does either latently or who are considerably more developed than he is. He's a cocky little guy who doesn't know what he has and how to handle it. Given enough patience and years of working, he could possibly become a good healer."

These comments upset me, for Mitchell's own Institute of Noetic Sciences in California acted as the contracting agent for the Uri Geller experiments, and today there is no one as publicity-struck as the young Israeli psychic. Kraft's own statement regarding Mitchell's attack was one of anger. He said, "I'm going to tell you something that I've never told anyone before. It's that people just don't realize how—hard this is. How it feels when someone comes to you, twenty-six years of age and dying of cancer . . . someone your own age, and you see his twenty-one-year-old wife crying because they've exhausted medical science and there's nothing more then can do. How hard it is to see death in front of you—to feel what they are feeling and how it feels when you try to help them. And how it feels when you can't. Let Ed Mitchell worry about publicity. When you face death as often as I have, you don't worry about the exposure. I want the publicity because I want to treat thirty people a day. I can do it. I have the energy. I want to build records on thousands of cases. I want to keep healing until I prove that what I am doing exists."

In one respect Ed Mitchell is right—there *are* thousands of people in our country who are healers but don't even realize that they have this energy. Too bad, because group healing is most effective. With a group of people concentrating their energies toward an ill person, seeming miracles can be accomplished. In many instances the recipient of the healing does not even have to be in the room. I saw group healing accomplished on some American Indian reservations with truly amazing success. The medicine man leads the group that he has gathered into almost hypnotic states of consciousness as they work up their energy and direct it toward one of the tribe who is not well. Group healing was always a part of the psychic development classes I have held at different times over the years. And even when there was little success in other psychic development areas, the healing was always fruitful.

How exciting it would be to have group healing

done on a large scale. To have an entire community work on those people who are in the local hospital. In many instances patients would get better, or have at least some improvement. And as the media and publishing industry dig deeper into the investigative areas of healing, more and more people are becoming aware that they do indeed possess the ability to use their energies for healing.

One such person is Ann Valukis, an unassuming mother of three children who resides in Boston. As Ann became more interested in psychic phenomena, she became aware that she possessed healing ability. At first she didn't believe it, but psychics kept telling her that she did. An astrologer informed her that it was in her chart. Palmists, aura readers, and others kept telling Ann Valukis that she had a healing energy around her.

She read about healing, studied the various writing on the subject, and attended lectures and seminars. It wasn't long before she began to do psychic healing, at first on members of her own family or close friends. It worked: many were healed or helped in some way.

I asked Ann to tell me of an experience that was typical of her healing capability. She afforded me this answer:

"One of the most rewarding experiences I have ever had took place in the spring of 1973 when I was contacted by the parents of a newborn child. They were acquaintances of mine. The baby, Timmy, had been born with a hyaline membrane. On top of the membrane was an air sack. Due to the problem, he had great difficulty in breathing. The attending doctor was most concerned about Tim and told his parents that it was touch and go; if the child lived, it would take as long as six months to dissolve the membrane. His mother called me and asked me to do psychic healing for Timmy.

"I began work for the child and would repeat these sentences throughout the day: 'Timmy, your physical disturbance is being freed; your condition is clearing up; you are well and healed *now*! When I was doing my housework, I would talk to Timmy as though he were close by and a grown person. I constantly told him that he had to get well, that he had to live. I would picture his chest with a fire or flames burning away the sac on his chest. Then I would close my eyes and picture him drenched in the healing rays of purple light.

"I continued this for a week, day and night, repeating it over and over. About a week later his mother phoned me and said that the doctor had taken X rays that showed the sac on the top of the membrane was gone. Several days later, another X ray revealed that the entire membrane had dissolved. We were delirious with joy. The delighted doctor said that it was a miracle and told the parents that God had been good to them, for he had not seen this kind of an outcome for Timmy.

"Timmy came home and seemed to be okay. But

a few weeks later he wouldn't eat, refused to nurse, and did not gain any weight. Again I began to work for him, to send him energy all day, every day. I talked to Timmy as though he were with me and understood what I was saying. I would tell him to eat, for that was the only way that he could stay on the earth plane and complete the karmic pattern of his life in this existence.

"Another week passed. Again Timmy's mother called. This time she asked me what I was doing, because suddenly the child was unable to get enough food. He wanted to nurse all the time, and his mother couldn't keep up with him. But he gained the correct weight. What I know I did was to surround Timmy with loving vibrations, continuously sending him light and healing. He is now a healthy two year old. Medical science cannot understand the healing, that it was so rapid and so very complete."

Improving Your Own Personal Vibrations

We are like television sets. At times we will get a full clear picture of what kind of vibrations are being sent us. At other times, the vibrations will be hazy, unclear, indistinct. This could be due to a fault in our own receptive ability, or in that which is transmitting the energy. Like a good TV set, we must work to keep our pictures clear by keeping it in top running condition, by keeping the energy flowing and by "tuning in" to the many various programs on the many different stations.

I have discovered a certain place that actually brings up the vibratory level of anyone visiting it, even those who are not particularly aware. Not too far from my home in the Catskill Mountains is a township called Big Indian. In this town is a restaurant called Rudi's Big Indian, a rather large building, one side of which is enclosed by a huge greenhouse. The rest of the complex consists of a restaurant with an adjoining outdoor patio. It is decorated very simply in country style: unfinished wood, high beams, much window glass to look out of. There are Southeast Asian artifacts on the walls.

Friends had recommended that I try this restaurant. They told me only that it was run by some people in a spiritual commune, but that the food was great "just the same." Without any other information, I happened into the restaurant one day while riding past it. The instant I entered the building, I sensed an overpowering feeling of peace, tranquillity, and "good."

This feeling was borne out by the hostess and then the waiters. They exuded a feeling of warmth, actually caring for their customers as people instead of the usual waiterly manner of treating patrons as so many dollar bills. Ironically, the vibratory level of the place puts off many people who do not know what they are unconsciously picking up; consequently, they react to the good vibes with either a form of bewilderment or inferiority.

Everything from the service to the decor exudes a vibration of love and care. For me, going to Rudi's is like taking an ocean voyage on which the entire crew and passengers are involved in meditation and metaphysics. The vibes are that overpowering.

The food at Rudi's was great the first time I ate there, and it has never failed to be the same. I would class it as one of the best restaurants I have ever eaten in—and that includes all of the United States, Europe, and the Orient. Nor is this a commercial—the restaurant doesn't need it. It's always jammed.

The restaurant was started by Albert Rudolph, an American who, after having met two Tibetan lamas who introduced him to the teachings of Buddha, set out on an inner awareness search at the age of six. Upon graduating college, the young man studied at the Gurdjieff Institute inNew York City for some five years and for a time lived with the guru Shankaracharya of Puri. This learned and holy man opened up many doors of awareness for Rudolph, who then went into the Oriental art and antiques business and later opened a school for teaching the higher aspects of spiritual life.

He became Swami Rudananda (also known as Rudi) and soon had fourteen schools in the United States and three in Europe. It was Rudi's idea to bring together a group of people who could work together in a positive, peaceful manner and contribute something to the world by utilizing this productive, positive energy that he himself had sought and learned to harness. By contrast, most communes tend to become closed off from society, teaching that only those in the commune will survive and that they must be protective of and productive for only those in their group.

In the early 1970s Rudi was killed in a plane crash. Those who had been close to him decided to continue his work, utilizing the energy he created. Besides the restaurant, the group is involved in a florist business and a construction company, both successful. The group who live at Rudi's meditate twice daily. The energy that Rudi created is still very much alive and kept so by those who strive to build the vibrations there every day. The radiation of love and human compassion that emanates from each and every person is a part of Rudi's Big Indian.

On two occasions, Rudi's vibrations were put to the supreme test, so to speak. Against my better judgment, I took a friend there who is a downer in the complete sense of the word. She is a negative person who is so sad that it can break your heart to be around her. Nothing ever pleases her, nothing is ever right or good enough for her. No matter where you go, this woman's vibrations are so overpoweringly negative that they cancel any positive energy in the atmosphere.

True to fashion, Rudi's restaurant proved no different. Everything seemed to go wrong. There was only a skeleton crew, as most of the help were on a spiritual retreat, and the service was not up to par. The soup was slightly cold. The meal was a bit too spicy. The famous dessert—truly an act of love by the baker who does all her work in a sub-basement that becomes as hot as a sauna—was not on the menu that day.

For a moment I had felt that the place must have gone the way of all good, positive things. But then I realized who I was with. I don't believe that it was coincidental that this was the time I chose to take this lady to Rudi's. Her negative vibrations were very much in evidence.

No matter when we would have gone, we would have had a bad time. I have not had another experience like that at Rudi's, and I have been going there for years.

On another occasion, one of several people I had taken to Rudi's for lunch became quite uptight the moment we walked in. I hadn't let this person know anything about Rudi's before we went there, other than it was a fine restaurant. The instant we were seated in the large, quite enchanting dining room, this particular woman said that she felt ill at ease.

This lady had dodged any form of spiritual

enlightenment as anyone else would the plague. She cannot even stand to talk about awareness or the more evolved aspects of life. She lives in constant fear of these things, and like most people who are afraid of something, she will strike out at anything that might tend to confirm her prejudice.

"What's the matter with this place?" my guest demanded when we were seated. "It's really odd here. The people seem odd to me. The room is strange."

"Everything's fine," I tried to reassure her.

"Oh, no, it isn't," she insisted. "I have the impression that the people who work here are looking at me, laughing at me. I don't know what it is that I feel, but they seem to be haughty or something."

Her reaction fascinated me. In truth, the woman had zeroed in on the vibrations of Rudi's. She could not stand the unconscious knowledge she was picking up of the very highly evolved awareness. Her conscious mind was translating the perfect vibes of Rudi's as negative ones. I had really thought that the vibes of Rudi's would somehow bring her up, but she interpreted them as being entirely unsympathetic and therefore "bad." She kept up the barrage of self-destructive hatred to the point that we merely had coffee and a piece of cake and then left.

This woman could not cope with the energy that was and is still very much a part of Rudi's. She could not comprehend the love that permeates the place. When I informed her of Rudi's background, she looked at me and said, "No *wonder* I felt there was

174

something wrong with them. It was like the same feelings I get whenever I read or even think about Charles Manson and his family."

How very wrong the lady was! This proves that what we can sense of an energy is often in direct ratio to our own awareness or enlightenment. That is why it is so important to build up our energies in positive ways. As D. in my development class put it, "That is why it is so very important to build up the positive vibrations around you all the time to tune in to the positive vibrations that are in the world. That's what metaphysical religions in actuality do. They make the person practicing metaphysics aware of the positive vibrations of persons, places, or things; and in so doing, open up positive vibratory forces around themselves. Religious Science, Christian Science, Unity, and others work on the assumption that there are positive vibrations around each of us, and to utilize these good vibrations for oneself and those around us, all one has to do is to recognize them, tune in to them, and accept them."

"Babies give off vibrations too," V. said, "and I always can sense them. They have not had a chance to clutter up their aura with life and their auras seem to glow." When I was on Harbour Island, one morning after breakfast, I took a stroll around the island. Children were out in force that day, I called my hellos to them. One particularly charming boy jumped off his bicycle to greet me.

"Hi," I said to him.

"Hello," the youth beamed a happy response.

"What's your name?" I asked him.

"My name is Michael," he replied in a thick Bahamian accent, British in quality but more carefully enunciated.

"It's a beautiful day, isn't it, Michael?" I exclaimed, glancing up at the cottonlike cumulus clouds which forever seem to hover over Harbour Island, endlessly forming themselves into castle towers, huge animals, or vast mountain ranges.

"Yes, it is a most beautiful day," Michael answered.

"How old are you?" I inquired.

"I am eight going on nine years old," the youth replied.

I could see that Michael wanted more conversation, so I asked him the inevitable question: "What do you want to be when you grow up?"

A fireman, a policeman, a politician—one of those answers I would have expected. But the lad put his hand up to his head, thought for a brief moment, and then said, "Michael."

His response threw me off guard. Michael's reply had not been made in an offhand, unthinking manner; nor was he being a smart aleck. The simple fact was that Michael wanted to be Michael when he grew up—nothing more, nothing less than a grown-up version of himself.

I had heard the replies to this question answered by countless children not only in America but throughout the world. The response is usually quick and to the point. Ask any child what he or she wants to be, and most often the answer will be not only a stated profession but the *top* of that profession, the *best* in that profession. Most of our children seem to have set goals before they are ten years old. What had been so startling in Michael's response was his complete lack of any materialistic objective. This freedom from material desire, I discovered, was an integral part of the psychological makeup of almost all the people I encountered during my stay.

For about a year after my return from the Bahamas, I would ask children I came into contact with what they wanted to be. The majority of them offered immediate responses to the question. No matter how young, American children for the most part seem to have their minds set on becoming someone very important when they grow up, and usually very wealthy.

"Why do you want to be a doctor?" I asked one child of about nine. I had hoped that within the boundary of his response there would be some feeling of human compassion for suffering.

"Well"—the child cocked his head, thinking about how he should answer—"I can make people better and I can get a lot of money and see lots of things in the world."

Alice wanted to be a drum majorette, a desire that seems to crop up quite often in young American girls, who for some reason, do not know that being a drum majorette is not a profession. "Why do you want to be a drum majorette?"

"So's that I can wear pretty clothes and so's that people can watch me and clap for me when I do it. I want to wear pretty, shiny clothes like all the drum majorettes."

"Do you think that it might make people happy to watch you when you twirl the baton?" I asked the seven-year-old.

"I don't know" was her answer.

A most common response from young American boys was "I want to walk on the moon." This was when moon walking and exploring were still being afforded the overemphasis it garnered in the late 1960s.

"Why do you want to walk on the moon?" I asked.

Typical of the answer was this reply from a ten-year-old New Yorker: "Because it's exciting to go on the moon and lots and lots of people will watch me on television . . . and then I can be in parades and all that."

On the other hand, several youngsters had different answers to my question. These were from the children of parents who had some background in spiritual enlightenment. Their responses were markedly different from those children whose parents were not involved in inner awareness.

"I would like to do something for people who are not happy, or are poor, or don't have anything" was the answer of a nine-year-old whose parents' were into the teachings of Buddha and the disciplines of yoga.

"I don't know yet. Whatever God wants me to be, I guess" was the reply of a young boy whose mother is an astrology teacher in Woodstock, New York.

"I want to be a scientist," said one young girl whose parents were students of Gurdjieff.

"Why?" I asked.

"Well, maybe I can help those many people who have cancer, or find some way to feed lots of people who are now hungry in the world, who don't have any food."

I made a study of these children whose parents were "on the path," exposing themselves to some form of higher teachings. I watched them at play and in their reactions to their parents. I was able to compare them with other children who had no basic spiritual background. There was a vast difference.

Children whose parents were involved in the positive, spiritual aspects of life were more "up," far happier, and better adjusted than their contemporaries who desired to be "the best astronaut" or "the most important businessman" or "a famous, rich television star." Childish squabbling was far less severe and they were much more giving, less selfish. Most importantly, something I hope that the medical profession of our country might make note of, these children were healthier! They had fewer colds, and, percentage-wise, did not acquire half the number of childhood diseases that other children did who had no understanding whatsoever of spirituality.

The vibrations of children with some awareness of the meaning of soul evolvement were decidedly different from those who had little or no exposure to the higher teachings. The auras were brighter and their energy level was much more pronounced.

Down in the Bahamas, Michael is now growing into a mature version of himself. Ralph, the young man whose vibrations attract so many large numbers of people, will no doubt become a singer with a vast admiring audience. Marilyn Monroe, who was forced into negating and hiding her true vibrations, denying (through a make-believe world that she chose to live in) the sensitive soul that she was, ultimately was destroyed. There is no doubt in my mind that vibrations must be considered above the physical and mental aspects of life.

One of the questions asked Dr. Stanley was "Can we change the vibrations in our individual auras? If so, what would be the most positive way in accomplishing this?"

Dr. Stanley: To build the proper vibratory energy field around oneself, an aura that consists of the highest, most pure energy, the physical, mental, and spiritual aspects of one's being must be brought into proper alignment. These three aspects of life make up what I shall term the divine triangle. And these aspects must be considered equally . . . one must not indulge himself in the progress of one at the expense of the other. It is just as harmful to place all your efforts and concentration on the spiritual and let the physical take care of itself as it is to do nothing at all. If one side of the triangle is neglected, the other two sides will be weakened and eventually collapse.

Question: Well, what then would be the most ideal way of building up the physical aspect of our lives in regards to positive vibrations, the auras which surround us?

Dr. Stanley: First and foremost is the diet. Improper diet is the physical cause of most illness, although the mental and spiritual aspects must be taken into consideration as well. Specifically, the aura is affected by the foods that are ingested. Natural foods must be eaten whenever possible. The proper natural foods will offer support to the divine triangle. It builds the mind which in turn makes it possible to accept the teachings of the spirit.

Question: You mean that there is some kind of diet that will be of importance to us spiritually?

Dr. Stanley: Exactly. First and foremost, there must be a proper balance of acidity and alkalinity in the body. Too much acidity will cause major physical breakdowns in the body, illnesses. This often shows in the auras of those who ingest large amounts of acid-creating foods—the aura tends to vibrate a muddy-yellow-gray color. Foods that combine fats with sugars are the worst offenders of the acid-forming foods. Cakes, baked goods, and candy should be eliminated altogether. Products made with processed white flour combined with sugar are the main causes of physical body breakdowns. The cells of the body are poisoned by the acid that this combination makes in the system. Ice cream is not as bad, but the best dessert is uncooked fruit. The majority of people believe that citrus fruit causes acidity in the system. This is completely false! They do not of themselves produce acid in the body. Sugars combined with fats create acidity. The natural acids in fruit help to break down the fats and sugars in the body.

Question: Are there any foods that should be avoided?

Dr. Stanley: Milk should not be taken after the age of twenty-one, unless it is a skim milk product. Milk is not needed by adults and it leads to sinus and gall bladder conditions and overcalcification of the bones. Arthritis can result from the ingestion of milk in an adult system. If parents would not give any milk to children during the cold or flu season, their children would stand a much better chance to ward off the infections. Those people who indulge themselves in fatty, creamy, or fried foods—such as what is called "quick foods"—have unclear auras. They vibrate a dull color, usually a grayish hue. When you are developing the ability to read or sense vibrations, check the aura of a friend or relative who eats mostly in quick-food restaurants. You will see that they do indeed have muddy auras. Compare this with someone who eats mostly fresh foods such as

Japanese food, which consists mainly of fish and vegetables. You will see that the auras of these people are clear as to color, never a faded shade of the color of their individual aura. The rich starch- and sugar-loaded food such as that eaten by the French people creates many health problems, and the aura is consequently vibrated at a very low level.

Question: What about meat? There have been many pros and cons regarding the ingestion of meats.

Dr. Stanley: Those who indulge themselves in meat as their main source of food have reddish auras—they vibrate the sensuality and the emotional aspects that too much meat will produce. On the other hand, it is important to have meat in the diet at least four or five times every week. Lean meats do indeed offer proteins that cannot be got from any other foods. The *complete* vegetarian diet is a negative one for the building of vibrations. Meat should not be eliminated from the diet, but it should be taken with care, not every day . . . and certain meats should not be eaten. Pork is bad because of the high fat content. Lamb that is fatty should not be ingested; in fact, the fat that comes from lamb is far worse for the health than even pork. Meat should never be eaten with any sugar or starch foods, only vegetables.

Question: You mentioned milk as not being good for health under certain circumstances. What about other dairy foods?

Dr. Stanley: Cheese is a good substitute for milk, but only the natural white cheeses, never the processed cheese. Plain, untreated yogurt is very good for health, but only two or three times a week. Too much milk, too many dairy products causes calcification that builds up, and many arthritic problems do arise from this. If milk products are necessary in conditions such as ulcers, then the patient must take vitamin D which breaks down the calcification.

Question: What about processed foods?

Dr. Stanley: Processed foods should not ever be ingested. Chemically treated foods do cause cancer. The natural chemistry of the cells is broken down by the added chemicals (there are, of course, mental and spiritual attitudes that must be considered in disease such as cancer, but food does play a major role in the creation of such illnesses). Overprocessed and foods that have additives should be eliminated from the diet altogether.

Question: Is there anything more you can tell us about food in regards to building a healthy aura?

Dr. Stanley: Yes, coffee is not good in quantity, and this would mean more than one cup per day. It is addictive and there is a residual effect with the caffeine. This builds up the chances for nervous disorders. It would amaze you how many diseases would clear up if the ingestion of coffee were stopped. And it is important to take note that just as many diseases are caused by processed sugars. Sugar in its natural state, such as honeys, fruits that contain sugar, is ample and enough. Low blood sugar is affecting many of your children, and that is why they are cranky, nervous, and become ill at so young an age. Throughout the day one should have seeds, especially sunflower or pumpkin seeds, or nuts such as almonds, to replace the craving for something sweet to snack on. As these natural foods become more and more popular, many of those suffering from various diseases will become well.

Question: We have talked quite a bit about the physical aspect of the divine triangle, and it is appreciated. What about the mental and the spiritual aspects that would help us to vibrate more positively?

Dr. Stanley: In the mental realms, discipline and the immersion of one's mind in one of the metaphysical teachings is the best way to build correct vibrations for the individual. To constantly work at seeing the positive in those around you and the incidents that befall you. Difficult, but not impossible. As one grows in metaphysics, the body improves, warding off sickness. The divine triangle is reinforced by the mental attitude of an individual. The spiritual aspects must also be brought into one's frame of reference. To be aware spiritually is the most important of all, for it is through one's spiritual evolvement that future incarnations will be based. The type of awareness development varies from one person to the next. It is therefore impossible to suggest where to go for spiritual awareness, but meditation is the best route. Yoga improves body, mind, and spirit and that is why it is so complete. Some religions such as Buddhism teach the same, that there must be serious work done on the physical as well as the mental planes of experience. If one truly seeks, the way is made open. The process of awareness seeking may vary, but those who have given themselves to doing this have bright, clear auras and therefore give off vibrations that are of the highest, most pure nature.

Index

Children, wishes of, 176-80
China, 85, 140
Clicks, lock, 161-64
Cocteau, Jean, 124
Coffee, 184
Coincidence, 124-38
Colds, 182
Color in auras, 108-15, 117-22
   food and, 181-83
Communication, nonverbal,
   55
Cooper, Alice, 95-96
Curse, healing compared to,
   150

Dali, Salvador, 102-4
Daugherty, Allen, 61
Death
   vibrations after, 60-62
   vibrations of, 136-38
Decyanin, 43
Dent, Eileen, 151-55
Dent, Roxanne, 69
Deschamps, Monsieur, 128-29
Diet, proper, 181-85
Di Maio, Dr. Dominick, 136-37
Disease (illness)
   diagnosis of, by auras, 44
   diet and, 181-85
Divine triangle, 180-81, 185
Dr. Stanley (author's trance
   consciousness), 45-46,
   180-86
Donovan, 95
Dreams, 17-19, 21, 130-31

Drug addicts, auras of, 120
Drugs, 97, 99
Duke University's Institute for
   Parapsychology, 135-36
Dutch settlers, 142

Ecclesiastes, 124
Egypt
   pyramids of, 83-84
   sacred books of, 40
   Tutankhamen's tomb in,
      84-85, 140
Epilepsy, aura of, 44
Etheric body, 44
Evers, Alf, 142

Fats, 181-82
Flammarion, Camille, 128
Flu, 182
Fort Lee (N.J.), 12
Fortgibu, Monsieur de, 128-29
Frank, Gerold, 112
Fruit, 182

Gall bladder conditions, 182
Garland, Judy, 108-15, 118
Geier, Buddy, 161-63
Geller, Uri, 164
Gene, 78-83, 140
Geography, vibrations and, 9,
   78-91
   See also Homes
Ghost stories, 60-62, 140

191